Opimōtēwina wīna kapagamawāt

WĪTIGŌWA

Journeys of The One to Strike the

WETIGO

Opimōtēwina wīna kapagamawāt

WĪTIGŌWA

—————◇—————

Journeys of The One to Strike the

WETIGO

KEN CARRIERE

Printed and bound in Canada at Imprimerie Gauvin. The text of this book is printed on 100% post-consumer recycled paper with earth-friendly vegetable-based inks.

COVER AND TEXT DESIGN: Duncan Noel Campbell
COPY EDITOR: Dallas Harrison
PROOFREADER: Rachel Taylor
COVER PHOTO: Ken Carriere's father, Pierre Carriere (right), and friend Paul Dussion with a 160-pound sturgeon caught on the Central Angling River in the Saskatchewan River Delta in the early 1960s. Carriere had caught the sturgeon, and Dussion had helped to land it. At far left, looking toward the camera, is Ken's older brother Franklin, who had found someone with a camera to photograph the record catch. Photo by Anne Hunter (née Nesbitt) of Prince Albert, Saskatchewan, courtesy of Les Carriere, Cumberland House.

Library and Archives Canada Cataloguing in Publication

TITLE: Opimōtēwina wīna kapagamawāt Wītigōwa = Journeys of The One to Strike the Wetigo / Ken Carriere.

OTHER TITLES: Journeys of The One to Strike the Wetigo

NAMES: Carriere, Ken, 1951- author.

DESCRIPTION: Includes bibliographical references. | Includes some text in Swampy Cree.

IDENTIFIERS: Canadiana (print) 20220400628 | Canadiana (ebook) 20220400687 | ISBN 9780889779075 (hardcover) | ISBN 9780889779044 (softcover) | ISBN 9780889779051 (PDF) | ISBN 9780889779068 (EPUB)

SUBJECTS: LCSH: Carriere, Ken, 1951—Childhood and youth. | LCSH: Carriere, Ken, 1951-—Family. | CSH: First Nations—Hunting—Saskatchewan. | CSH: First Nations—Trapping—Saskatchewan. | CSH: First Nations—Fishing—Saskatchewan. | CSH: First Nations—Saskatchewan—Social life and customs. | CSH: First Nations—Saskatchewan—Biography. | LCGFT: Autobiographies.

CLASSIFICATION: LCC E99.C88 C37 2022 | DDC 971.24/2004973230092—dc23

10 9 8 7 6 5 4 3 2 1

University of Regina Press

University of Regina, Regina, Saskatchewan, Canada, S4S 0A2
TEL: (306) 585-4758 FAX: (306) 585-4699
WEB: www.uofrpress.ca

We acknowledge the support of the Canada Council for the Arts for our publishing program. We acknowledge the financial support of the Government of Canada. / Nous reconnaissons l'appui financier du gouvernement du Canada. This publication was made possible with support from Creative Saskatchewan's Book Publishing Production Grant Program.

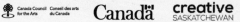

To all the Cree, Dene, and Métis people who continue to enjoy the land. May we continue to live on this planet, Mother Earth, by not destroying what it has provided for us in the past. May we leave a healthy place for the unborn who are scheduled to arrive.

CONTENTS

———————◇———————

PART 2: DROP BY, DON'T BE A STRANGER

ACKNOWLEDGEMENTS

———————◇———————

Thanks to Nigāwiy, my mother, Nora Agnes Carriere, affectionately known as Sōminis, and to Nohtāwiy, my father, Pierre Carriere Sr., known as Chi Pierre.

To Nimisak, my older sisters: Anne Carriere-Acco, who helped me to get a BSc degree, provided family photos and history, and, as a writer, gave me literary advice; and Verna Wendt, who also helped me to get my BSc degree and gave me family photos. Verna worked as a certified nurse's assistant in both Montreal and Ottawa.

To Nistīsak, my older brothers. To Franklin, who gave me stories about our father on the trapline and who, thankfully, took photos of elders. Franklin continued our uncle Roger Carriere's tradition of participating in King Trapper competitions in northern Saskatchewan and Manitoba, and he competed in canoe racing with his partner, Napoleon Laliberte, including at the 1967 Centennial Canoe Pageant—Franklin with Team Saskatchewan and Napoleon with Team Northwest Territories. Franklin still hunts and traps, teaches trapping essentials, and entertains at King Trapper events. He and his wife, Penny, helped me to get a BEd degree through the University of Regina and University of Saskatchewan doing course work through the Northern Teacher Education Program in La Ronge. My brother John gave me stories of our father of our grandfathers, Leonile and Dougal, as well as stories of Elders Stephen Jake (Sēpincēk) Greenleaf and Nathan Settee. Today John doesn't practise on-the-land activities as he once did, but he does provide valuable advice to new trappers, fishers, and hunters. He inherited the two tourist camps that our father operated, and his son Ryan now runs the one on the Mossy River.

To Nisīm, my younger sister, Donna Mirasty, who helped at home when our father's health was failing. She works as a certified nurse's assistant. Donna kept family photos and graciously shared them with me.

To Nisīmisak, my younger brothers. To Clifford, with whom I hunted and snared rabbits when we were children; we also trapped squirrels and weasels. Clifford still runs his own trapline. He raced dog teams in winter festivals and taught his children hunting, camping skills, dog racing, running, and canoe racing. He grows wild rice, and as a school teacher he enjoys teaching Cree and outdoor education. To Les, with whom I have hunted ducks and geese many times, an annual late-fall event. Les is a journeyman carpenter, and he stays connected with the trade unions since he believes in the benefits that they provide for working men and women. He has held jobs in many work sites throughout Saskatchewan. Les fishes commercially, hunts, traps, and guides hunters whenever he is not on a job site. He is also passionate about photographing wildlife.

To Nōkomak, my grandmothers: on my mother's side, Virginie Jourdain and Christiana Cursiteur (Custor); on my father's side, Agnes Morin.

To Nimosōmak, my grandfathers: on my mother's side, Dougal McKenzie; on my father's side, Leonile (or Lionel or Neonile) Carriere.

Acknowledgements

To Nitānskotāpānak, my great-grandparents: maternal great-grandfathers, Bill McKenzie and Louis Jourdain; maternal great-grandmothers, Jemima Hall and Marguerite McKay; paternal great-grandfathers, Isadore/Theodore Carriere, James Ballandine, and Antoinis Morin; and paternal great-grandmothers, Angelique Dorion (Nōtigē Āsalik), Veronique Merasty, and Rebecca (Ānipēga) Cowley.

To Kāgīcitēyicik, the big-hearted ones. These people, whether I knew them directly or not, had lives that nonetheless influenced me: John Budd, Stephen Jake Greenleaf, Moise Dussion, Ovide "Cheechip" Goulet, Joe and Virginia Morin, Alex Morin, Colin (Jackson) Cook, Daniel Cook, Sarah McAuley-Carriere (midwife), Johnny and Lena Stewart (midwife), Rod and Marie Louise McKay, Roderick and Melanie McKay, Chief Tom Settee and his wife, Adele Morin-Settee, Pat and Louisa Buck, Margaret McKenzie-McAuley (midwife), and Flora Settee-McAuley (midwife). Of course, others have been gifted with helpful skills and been kind enough to share them with others. This is how they built their communities.

To my great-uncles, my father's uncles: Albert (Ānipats) Flett and Joe Morin.

To my great-aunts: my mother's aunt, Mary McKenzie Warren, who came to live with my parents, and Adele Morin-Settee, my father's aunt.

To Nisisak (my uncles, my mother's brothers): Angus McKenzie (Amisk Lake), Rod McKenzie (Winnipeg), John McKenzie (The Pas), Bill "Steamboat" McKenzie (Cumberland House), and Simeon Bloomfield (Cumberland House); and to my father's sisters' husbands, Arthur "Archie" Goulet, John Morin, Hilliard McKenzie, and Simeon Sayese.

To Nohkomisak (my uncles, my father's brothers): step-brothers Isidore and Jonas Carriere; biological brothers Alphonse, William, James, and Roger Carriere; and to my mother's sisters' husbands, Joseph McAuley, Mike Dubinak, William Carriere, and Louis Nabess.

To Nitōsisak (my aunts, my mother's sisters): Ethel Nabess, Josephine Carriere, Kate Dubinak, and Margaret McAuley; and to my father's brothers' wives, Sarah McAuley-Carriere, Suzanne Michel, Helda Carriere, Josephine McKenzie, Margaret "Teapot" McKay, Caroline Stewart, and Olive Whitehead.

To Nisikosak (my aunts, my father's sisters): Veronique Goulet, Marie Alma Morin, Marie Louise McKenzie, and Elise Sayese; and to my mother's brother's wives, Florence Sayese and Maryanne Pelly.

To my parents' family friends and relatives. These people were permanent residents of Cumberland House and knew my parents well: Pat and Louisa Buck, Johnny and Lena Stewart, John and Nancy Thomas, Donald and Clara Carriere, Adolphe and Miriam Carriere, David and Alice Goulet, Jean Baptiste and Victoria Laliberte, John Dorion, Marie Dorion, Cecilia Dorion, William "Menjalie" and Isabelle Dorion, Joe T. and Ruby Dorion, Paul and Flora Dussion, Moise and Agnes Dussion, Baptiste and Marie Dussion, Charlie and Harriet Fosseneuve, Charlie and Christina Head, Joe Pelly, Joe and Virginia Morin, and George and Rosalie McAuley. If I have missed any couple or anyone, it is not intentional.

To the people who worked as government civil servants, in medical services, or in the religious order and were non-permanent residents. In the government of Saskatchewan civil service: James "Jim" Brady, Tommy Francis, Ron and Evelyn Mackay, Bert Johnson Don Neilson, Gilbert and Angelique McKay, Torrence Tornquist, and others. In the Nipawin Hospital: Doctors Bala and Fitton. With the Oblate Missionary Order: Father Trudeau, Father Chamberlain, Sister St. Remy, Sister St. Albert, and others.

To those who helped me to further my education, particularly the late Dr. Sydney Lumbers, curator of geology at the Royal Ontario Museum, Toronto. He introduced me to voyageur birchbark canoe builder Charlie LaBerge of Sturgeon Falls, Ontario, and gave me a chance to study the complex Precambrian geology of the Grenville Province along the Upper Ottawa River and in Algonquin Provincial Park. Dr. Lumbers provided me with an opportunity to study Precambrian geology and lunar samples at the University of Toronto and employed me as his assistant at the Royal Ontario Museum. This education led me to work for Parks Canada in Ottawa, when I first read the writings of Henry David Thoreau, published in the *Beaver Magazine* (now *Canada's History*), one of the reference magazines that Parks Canada had on hand.

I also wish to thank my friends Alan and Agathe Moar of Masteuiatsh (Pointe-Bleue) on the shores of Lac St-Jean, Quebec, for their friendship. Alan and his brothers Clifford and Gordon introduced me to their late father Kenny Moar's moose-hunting camp at Réserve faunique Ashuapmushuan (the Ashuapmushuan Wildlife Reserve). This is where the Moar family still practised their Cree way of living off the land in the northern boreal forest of Quebec.

Appreciation also to Jerry Polson, of Winneway First Nation in northwestern Quebec, who taught me Mother Earth teachings practised by the Anishinaabe and Algonquin. And to Canadian writers Tom Alderman, who introduced me to Snowbird Martin in the Weekend Edition of the *Winnipeg Free Press* in the 1960s, and later Andrew H. Malcolm, who wrote about Snowbird Martin in the *New York Times* in the 1980s. My gratitude also to Peter "Peechee" Ladouceur of the Wood Buffalo National Park Warden Service for introducing me to Snowbird Martin in the summer of 1976 at the Snowbird Settlement on the Athabasca River Delta.

And I must acknowledge Nitaskīnān (Our Home Land), the Saskatchewan River Delta, and all that lies within it, including the South, Central, and North Angling Rivers, the Mossy River, the Steamboat Channel, the Hudson's Bay Fur Lease, Snake Point, the Tearing River, the Bigstone River, Cumberland Lake, Belanger Lake, Barrier Lake, Cross Lake, Limestone Island, Pine Island, Muskeg Lake, Cīcīgamisihk (a muskeg shoreline at the north end of Cumberland Lake), Frog Island, Gun Creek, Blackmud Bay, and the Old Channel. And the northern rivers and lakes that drain into the delta basin: the Grassberry River, Windy Lake, Suggi Lake, Limestone Lake, Achininni Lake, Amisk Lake, Namew Lake, the Sturgeon-weir River, and Opāwakoscikan (Pelican Narrows), after which the northern village is named. Additionally, many places frequented by individuals were named after them, place names still used by locals; for example, Ēlin Cāwmasihk (Helen Thomas's Place), Anipachihk (Albert Flett's Place), and Lesiyihk (Les's Place). At Amisk Lake, there is also a place called Dougal's Island, where my grandfather Dougal McKenzie had his summer camp.

Last, but not least, I wish to express my appreciation to the Saskatchewan Arts Board for providing funds that helped to make this project possible. My grant application was made under the Independent Artists program, and in my "Artistic Vision/Artist Statement" I provided the following: "My goal is to establish a niche for myself where my writing in the Cree language will be part of literature." I hope that I have met this objective. With the funding, I was able to travel in east-central Saskatchewan and west-central Manitoba and to visit and interview relatives whose memories corroborated mine and the stories that I tell in this book. Their stories at times were very humorous but also gripping, filled with life's ups and downs. The interviews with Cree speakers were conducted in the Swampy Cree dialect; the interviews with non-Cree speakers were done in English only. My healthy relatives and friends still carry on with their land-based activities. They also teach the skills and knowledge needed to continue those activities. I am thankful that I was able to reach a generation of people who grew up before their world was invaded by modernism and morphed into full automation.

A NOTE ON THE SWAMPY CREE
USED IN THIS BOOK

◇

The Swampy Cree language I use in this book is the language I grew up with. It was passed down from generation to generation through oral tradition, and it makes us who we are. Our language was not meant to be written. The first publication of it using Standard Roman Orthography (SRO) was in the 1850s, a biblical translation. In this book, I have written the Cree language using that orthography, which uses macrons. I understand that they are used for non-Cree speakers who wish to practise speaking Cree. In my own Cree-writing experience, I am able to read the Cree wording without sounding it out to get the meaning, though during my writing I had to sound the words out to make them come alive. I also had to do that to ensure grammatically correct usage. My understanding is that in Saskatchewan and Alberta most Cree-language writing is done in SRO with the use of macrons. I have also provided approximate English translations of the Cree words and phrases, but I have discovered that translation of languages is tougher than what most people think. I have Cree grammars and dictionaries to check, and they help. There is also a guide to Swampy Cree pronunciations in the appendix on page 253 of this book.

The Swampy Cree language in the Cree writing community is known as the "N" dialect. In the Cree-speaking community, it is also known as the Cree that uses "g" instead of "k" for many Cree words. I only heard some other Cree dialect speakers describe it that way. So maybe that's good. They can still make out what we are talking about when we speak it our way. No need to discourage other Cree dialect speakers when the Cree language is losing speakers already. Although there might be some debate among people about some spellings, I am certain I will be understood by other Swampy Cree speakers. It is my hope that this book will help others interested in the language to learn it. What is important is speaking it and passing it on.

Map 1: The Saskatchewan River Delta, showing the distinct upper (western) and lower (eastern) regions and their interconnectedness with western Canada's major waterways.

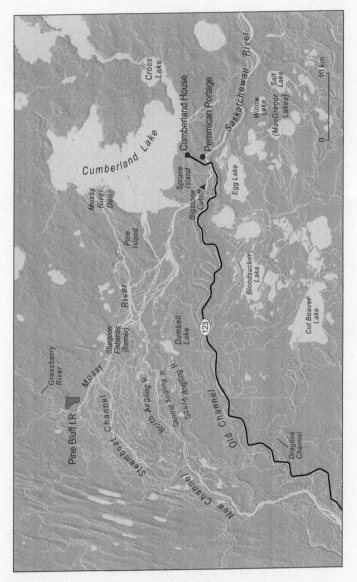

Map 2: The region of the continually changing upper (western) Saskatchewan River Delta to the west and south of Cumberland Lake.

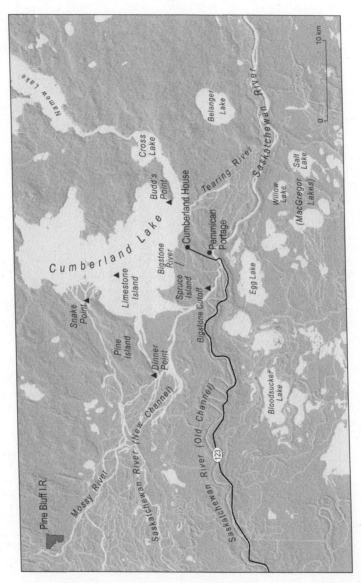

Map 3: Detail of the area surrounding Cumberland Lake.

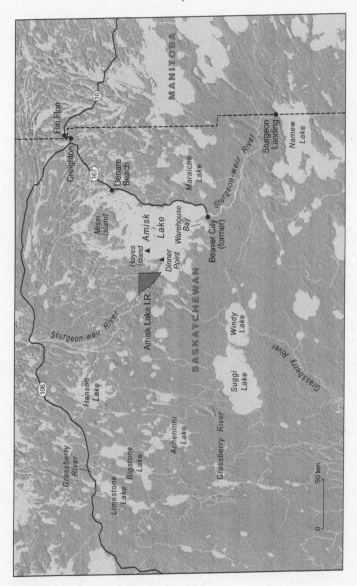

Map 4: Amisk Lake and Grassberry River regions.

INTRODUCTION

The recollections and travel memoirs in this book are based upon journeys with my relatives in the upper (or western) portion of the Saskatchewan River Delta, which along with the lower (or eastern) portion forms the largest inland delta in North America, covering approximately 10,000 square kilometres or close to 4,000 square miles. Straddling the border between Manitoba and Saskatchewan, the delta began forming about 10,000 to 11,000 years ago as the ice sheets of the last ice age receded. It is one of the most biologically diverse places on the continent, and it is composed of various wetlands, shallow lakes, active and abandoned river channels, and forests, representing one of the most unique landscapes on the planet. The vast tracts of peatland and coniferous and boreal forest support hundreds of species of plants and act as a vital natural storehouse for carbon and a buffer against climate change.

Indigenous Peoples have lived in the region for at least 7,000 years, and in Swampy Cree, my first language, their travels through the land are described in terms that fit the traveller's purpose, such as pimōtēwak (they are on a trip) or pimpiciwak (they are moving out to their trapline or to another home). We describe activities associated with one's livelihood or methods of securing sustenance with other terms, such as topagitawāw (gone out to set fishnets), towanīgēw (gone out trapping fur bearers), tohasayigēw (gone out hunting waterfowl), and tomācīw (gone out hunting moose). With regard to moose, a most sacred animal to us, the delta was once heavily populated with this ungulate, and at one time herds of woodland caribou were known to inhabit the delta's forested uplands. The region also provides habitat for millions of waterfowl and other migratory birds. The forests sustain many other mammals, including black bear, wolf, lynx, elk, and whitetail deer. Beaver, muskrat, mink, and otter thrive in the waterways' main channels, creeks, lakes, and marshlands, and the waterways also support many species of fish. As my brother John Victor Carriere once told me, "You know the land is rich when the top two to three inches of soil can support animals as small as a mouse to as big as a moose." John and the other people I write about and have interviewed for this book are Indigenous, but there are also a few Euro-Canadians and Americans who came to the region for sport or business reasons either private or public.

The early inspiration for writing stories of my folks and of their connection to the land was when I first read a piece by American writer and naturalist Henry David Thoreau in *The Beaver* magazine (now *Canada's History*) when I was a young man. Thoreau had been profoundly affected during three trips that he had taken with Penobscot guides into the wilds of Maine in the 1840s and 1850s, and he was keenly interested in how Native American culture was being affected, culturally and politically, by European settlement. I was taken with his passion to understand how the Indigenous Peoples of the North American boreal forest ("Indians," as he called them) and the moose could have such a deep ecological relationship. Thoreau had studied the travel journals of Alexander Henry the Elder and was fascinated with the content. Henry, born in New Jersey and getting his start in business as a merchant in Albany, New York, had ventured to the Northwest Territories, hoping to profit from the ever-expanding fur trade. His journeys took him into the Saskatchewan River Delta and then north to Namew Lake, Amisk Lake, and the community of Opāwakoscikan (Pelican Narrows), places connected by the Sturgeon-weir River, historically important since it linked the Saskatchewan River and Churchill River systems.

Situated in the centre of the Saskatchewan River Delta is the Indigenous settlement of Cumberland House, where I grew up in the 1950s and 1960s. Established by Samuel Hearne in 1774 as the Hudson's Bay Company's (HBC) first inland trading post, Cumberland House was a key transportation hub and supply depot for 150 years since waterways from the community led north and northwest to the fur-rich Churchill and Athabasca regions, east to Hudson Bay, and southwest onto the plains and the herds of bison that provided the pemmican that fed the fur-trading brigades. The name of our neighbouring community, Kiskāciwanohk (or Pemmican Portage), speaks to that part of history. Henry arrived there in the fall of 1775, and shortly thereafter he and his men built a trading post on Amisk Lake. He admired the resourcefulness of the Indigenous people he encountered, people willing to share their knowledge of a land that Thoreau considered Homeric and hostile. Besides being a great writer, Thoreau was an avid reader. His reading of *The Odyssey* sustained his literary life.

But there were certain social perceptions among Euro–North Americans of our Indigenous brothers and sisters. I heard my tāwī (dad) tell my gāwī (mom) that the Mistigōsiwak (French explorers) had a term for us. He told her that white people thought of our people as *les maudit sauvages* (the cursed or damned savages). When my mother heard the phrase, she immediately disagreed with its connotation.

In her strong opinion, we were not like that at all. She said that savages are people who kill for pleasure and out of hate. Thoreau himself had preferred the old French definition of *sauvage* or *salvage* (the latter derived from *silva*, the Latin term for wood or forest) as someone who is a forest dweller.

In my own early reading, I had come across the term "savage" in accounts written by the Jesuit missionaries in eastern North America. The Jesuits were sent to pacify the Indigenous Peoples living in both North America and South America to make way for Spanish, Portuguese, Dutch, French, and English colonialists, and they were determined to convert the Indigenous Peoples to Christianity. One story I read was of Father Jean de Brébeuf, a Jesuit whom the Indigenous Peoples of the St. Lawrence River despised and eventually killed. The Haudenosaunee (Iroqouian Peoples) had their own creation story and their own spiritual practices, so they strongly rejected what the Jesuits offered.

But regardless of what the Euro–North Americans called us, in our Swampy Cree language we call ourselves Sagāwiniwak (Bush Land People), and we call the Cree who live in the boreal shield Asinskāwiniwak (Rock Land People) and the Crees who live on the prairies Paskwāwiniwak (Meadow Land People). For the Crees who live in the Hudson Bay lowlands, the Swampy Cree name is Omuskegowak.

As for my people, the Swampy Cree, I hope that the accounts in this book will inform readers of an Indigenous way of life that existed and still exists long after the extensive fur trade era. Yes, there are fewer trappers, hunters, and fishers living off the land, and, yes, this livelihood can be passed on only by actual practitioners. My father, his brothers, and their friends and relatives all learned from my dad's father, Leonile (Neonile) Carriere, and elders such as Stephen Jake (Sēpincēk) Greenleaf and Dougal McKenzie. These elders took care of their people, ensuring that they lived productive and comfortable lives. As my brothers John and Franklin say, "Nobody suffers much when they have the know-how."

Fourth from the left, my mother Agnes as a teenager with her younger sister Josephine third from the left and her stepmother Christiana McKenzie (née Cursiteur) with her baby Lily and Christiana's sister Marie at the far right at the Amisk Lake Reserve.

Photo courtesy of niciwāmiskwīm (my cousin, my mother's sister's daughter) Margaret Schweitzer, Denare Beach, Saskatchewan.

In addition to these male role models, there were adoptive mothers such as Christiana Cursiteur, who helped to raise my mother and her siblings. Christiana taught them the skills of raising children; keeping animals; gardening; cooking meals; tanning moose hides; making moccasins, mitts, and parkas (all clothing with exact stitching); and in general living good, healthy lives. Several generations after those of Christiana Cursiteur, Dougal McKenzie, Leonile Carriere, Stephen Jake Greenleaf, and others such as Johnny Stewart, Helen Thomas, Agnes Morin, and Nora Agnes Carriere, there are still friends and relatives who spend time on the land and carry on their traditions. My brother John hopes that future generations will respect the rituals of showing humility and gratitude to their elders and that higher power who sustains the natural life.

With regard to these traditions, if people are looking today for American and Canadian Indigenous literature or art that speaks to them, it is now available ōta ōma askiy (from this land here). It is in drum songs, songs accompanied by string, wind, and electronic music, short stories and novels, storytelling, live theatre, motion pictures, video reproductions, and other media. Our drum songs help us to heal, our music makes us appreciate who we are, and our written stories give us identities and histories. Our artisans and craftspeople can make a living with images claimed by, and of, our people. Our motion pictures bring stories to life on screen; our musicians, singers, dancers, and actors make us proud. Our hunters, gatherers, trappers, and fishers still provide sustenance, and they remind us that our land is sacred. They quietly go about their business, but with immense resolve they say "we need to take care of our Mother Earth." Although there are planets orbiting other stars like our Sun that some imagine might one day support human colonies, it is hard to imagine they could sustain life as Earth does.

As I mentioned above, my intention in writing these recollections of my travels through the Saskatchewan River Delta (and occasionally beyond), and in assembling the interviews that comprise the second half of this book, is partially to commemorate a culture, to compose an ethnography, if you will, that will be of interest to both English-language and Cree-language readers. But it is also to pay homage to my ancestors, my living relatives, and all the people in the broader communities of the delta. Particularly, I wish to honour my late mother, Nora Agnes Carriere (née McKenzie), who grew up on the Sturgeon-weir Indian Reserve, and my late father, Pierre Carriere, who was raised at the Pine Bluff Indian Reserve.

I remember some things that my father told me about his childhood. He grew up in the bush (sagāhk) and is a sagāhkiwiniw, a bush person. Wherever the fur trading posts got set up, the bush people made their homes. My father's parents, Leonile Carriere and Agnes Morin, operated the Pine Bluff trading post for the Hudson's Bay Company.

Leonile was the fur buyer, and Agnes was the bookkeeper. Leonile never learned to read or write. He had great physical strength, with plenty of energy, doing the bull work of taking the trapping goods and supplies out to the trappers wherever they had their traplines. Agnes had attended the Indian Residential School at Lebret, in southern Saskatchewan, where she had learned to read, write, count, and run a household. My grandparents were a team who served the Hudson's Bay Company exceptionally well.

I also remember a comment my mother made while speaking of her grandfather, Louis Jourdain. Louis transported the HBC trade goods from Fort à la Corne to Green Lake on what was known as the Green Lake Trail. It was gruelling work with meagre living wages and no benefits. He got paid only after delivering the goods. He was one of the original transport drivers called teamsters. In my mother's view, he was a slave for the Hudson's Bay Fur Trading Company.

In this book, I also seek to highlight some of the changes that have occurred in the delta after the building of the mistigipahigana (huge hydroelectric power dams) on the South Saskatchewan and Saskatchewan Rivers. They have had an enormous impact on the region, the waterways and lands, the flora and fauna, and the traditional lives of the people who live there. My brother John witnessed the many changes hydro dams brought to the upper delta, and, as one who has lived as a trapper, fisher, hunting guide, and outfitter, he has given me many insights into their effects. Mostly retired now, John still gets out on the land whenever he can.

Indeed, change is inevitable, and there are now different ways that people can make a living wage, but there are vast areas that have been sacrificed for, or are increasingly at risk of, major industrial development. Just as the Saskatchewan River Delta has been profoundly affected by hydroelectric projects, so too has the Peace–Athabasca Delta been affected. That vital delta, however, also faces continuing threats from Alberta's oilsands industry. Mining of all kinds is reshaping vast landscapes.

But other factors are also affecting the natural environment and the ways that people live off the land. In northern Alberta, Saskatchewan, and Manitoba, in addition to hydro-electric projects and mines, there are developments of public access highways, railroads, cottage subdivisions, and growing communities.

Fortunately, however, nature can be resilient, and with care hopefully some features might not change much in the long run. The natural world might be disrupted, but it might not be gone forever—like the overwintering redpoll: some winters they might not be in your neighbourhood, but they might be enjoyed by someone else somewhere else, and they might return to your backyard in years to come.

In the first half of this book, the journeys I write of were with my late father, Pierre (Chi Pierre) Carriere Sr., and my late mother, Nora Agnes (Sōminis) Carriere; my late uncles James Carriere and John Morin; my late great-uncle Albert (Ānipats) Flett; my brothers Franklin, John, Clifford, and Les Carriere; and my cousins Philip (Red) Fosseneuve, Ordean and Mildred Goulet, and Gerald Morin. The travels were done by canoe and paddle, by motorized freighter canoes, by dog teams, by ski-equipped airplane, by fully covered snow tracker, and by vehicle. Two trips I mention involved my father's medical trips in the late 1970s: one to Oskana Kāsastēki (Pile of Bones, now Regina) for surgery in 1978, the other to Nipawin, where he was hospitalized in 1979.

Among the interviews that comprise the second half of this book are those that I conducted in Swampy Cree (or Cree "N" dialect) with my aunts Elise Sayese and Marie Louise McKenzie, my late father's sisters. For these interviews, I have provided English translations. Among other observations, my aunts speak of their brothers, my father, Pierre, and his brothers James and Alphonse, who had served in Europe during the Second World War, and another brother, William, a reservist in Halifax. My aunts tell of how they survived that conflict and what life was like for them upon their return.

I also include interviews conducted in English with my cousins Margaret Schweitzer and Glen Dubinak, who live at the northern village of Denare Beach on Amisk Lake, Saskatchewan. Their parents, Mike and Kate Dubinak, had a commercial fishing operation at Amisk Lake started by my aunt Kate's grandfather Bill McKenzie with her father, Dougal McKenzie. My cousins are connected to this Amisk Lake commercial fishing operation, and today it continues with Glen's family, also members of the Peter Ballantyne Cree Nation. They are the ones who connect me and my siblings to Amisk Lake, where, as I mentioned above, Alexander Henry the Elder set up his trading post 250 years ago.

My brothers John and Franklin had the most contact with my late father, whom we still call Dad as if he never died. As a youngster during the 1950s, Franklin travelled with Dad on the trapline. There was still no motorized travel at that time—getting around was by paddling a canoe or running a dog team. Later, freighter canoes with squared sterns for mounting outboard motors were adopted for times when there was open water, but dog teams were still used in the winter. Franklin also helped with commercial fishing and guiding the increasing numbers of hunters who came to the region. John also helped Dad with the trapping as well as the guiding and commercial fishing. Like my interviews with my aunts Elise and Marie Louise, my interviews with John and Franklin are in Swampy Cree and accompanied with English translations.

———◇———

As a young child, before I was allowed to venture out on the land, I was kept close to home. We lived in a small, isolated settlement on an island, the community of Cumberland House. This northern village is located off the southern end of Cumberland Lake and on the north-central shoreline of the island, which we call Kāministikominahikoskāk (Island of Many White Spruce). My home had an enclosed yard with a barbed wire fence. My father was a trapper, hunter, hunter's guide, outfitter, and commercial fisher, and he often spread his fishing nets out on our lawn. My mother was a homemaker who raised eight children. Unfortunately, she lost three children: a newborn child, a baby, and a toddler. She maintained two large gardens and kept a working horse named Doll in our yard and inside a stable during the winter months. Doll hauled firewood and water from the nearby Bigstone River's wooded shoreline. We had a large woodpile of sawed and split green aspen that we left to get sunbaked for our kitchen stove. We burned this wood all through the winter to early spring. My mother also tanned moosehides on the lawn and beside a building we called the warehouse.

The warehouse was a log building where numerous implements were stored and where we kept a pile of books for a family friend named James "Jim" Brady. I learned to read from these books. The collection included a dictionary and poetry written by the famous Pauline Johnson, originally from the Six Nations First Nation in Ontario. Along with Jim's books was an accordion, Dad's musical instrument. Dad had learned to play the piano at the home of his childhood friend, George Cotter, and then he learned to play the accordion for dances. Today I can listen to Cajun music played by Andrew Carriere with an accordion on YouTube that makes me imagine my father playing the accordion for a dancing crowd.

In addition to Jim Brady's books, my reading included the *Winnipeg Free Press*, which my dad received by mail from The Pas, Manitoba, when I was a boy. It was in the paper that

I was eight years old when this photo was taken. My mother is in the top right, and I am the fourth child from the front. The log building in the background, whitewashed with lime, is where I would spend time in the attic reading from a pile of books, newspapers, and weekend magazines ordered from the *Winnipeg Free Press* and stored there.

Photo courtesy of Anne Carriere-Acco, Montreal, Quebec.

I first read of Napoleon "Snowbird" Martin in a story written by journalist Tom Alderman in 1968. Snowbird was a prominent and influential elder of the Mikisew Cree First Nation who lived at what is still known as Snowbird's Settlement on the Athabasca River between Fort McMurray and Fort Chipewyan in far northeastern Alberta. I had the good fortune to meet Snowbird and his family in the summer of 1976. He and his wife were elderly by then, but they still had the energy to enjoy the land with their grandchildren.

I greatly admired Tom Alderman for having written about Snowbird Martin, and later, while conducting research for this book, I found another story about Snowbird written by Andrew H. Malcolm published in the *New York Times* in

1981. Snowbird was seventy-seven years old then and running dogsled excursions out of Fort Chipewyan into Wood Buffalo National Park in northern Alberta and the Northwest Territories, and he gave the journalist, then thirty-seven, and his seven-year-old son Spencer an adventure tour worth a write-up in that esteemed newspaper.

I found that I wanted to write stories about people like Snowbird, so I put this book together to provide a glimpse of the bushland peoples of northern Canada and to share their knowledge of living in a forever-changing environment. In doing so, my only wish is that the inland deltas of northern Canada, or any other special places on this planet, don't just become industrial wastelands. Snowbird and my dad lived the bushland life. They were both excellent moose hunters, fishers, and trappers, and both helped to build a community of forest dwellers. May their memorable lives be carried on.

Part 1

ON THE LAND
AND IN THE SKY

OF WETIGOS AND WAR

◇

They said the man was fearless. His journeys took him from his island home, the place they call Kāministikominahikoskāk (Spruce Island). He would travel with white-capped waves on Cumberland Lake. Sometimes the waves crested at ten feet in the deepest parts of the lake. He would drive his twenty-foot freighter canoe powered by a ten-horsepower outboard motor with no hesitation. In the winter, he would leave at forty degrees below zero with high winds swirling and drifting snow. He trusted his lead dog to take him home or back to his trapline. He was a traveller like his father and forefathers, who lived off the land. I knew this traveller; he was my father. He took me on many trips for a reason that he mentioned to his friend: "Ēwako awa kapagamawāt Wītigowa" ("This one is to strike the Wetigo").

When I told my brother Les that I was writing about my travels with our late father, he wanted to know what I planned on calling the book. I said "Journeys of The One to Strike the Wetigo," which translated in Cree is "Opimōtēwina wīna kapagamawāt Wītigōwa." When Les asked me, "How

Pierre Carriere Sr. with a twenty-foot freighter canoe equipped with a ten-horsepower outboard motor.

Photo courtesy of Donna Mirasty, La Ronge, Saskatchewan.

come such a title?" I said, "I was on a boat trip with Dad when he stopped to greet [ēgīnagawāt] his friend [otōtēma], David 'Cheechigana' Goulet. David asked him 'Awina awa kāpōsiyat?' ['Who is this in your boat?'] And Dad replied, 'Ēwako awa ēpēsiwak kapagamawāt Wītigōwa.' ['I brought him along to strike the Wetigo.']" My father and his friend both chuckled after that comment. They had known each other for years and were sharing a joke—that this young boy (I would have been about ten) could be their protector.

I had first heard about the Wetigo as a child, and my mother had warned us about it. If we were playing out of our yard in the evening, she told us to come home before dark. She warned us of a Wetigo who came at night looking for children to take away. We listened to her. There was no telling what a Wetigo could do to you, just the cruellest and most horrible things imaginable.

When I was about eight years old, during the early spring as the daylight hours got longer at the fifty-fourth parallel, I went with friends, the brothers Lloyd and Harvey Young and their cousins Earl Cook and Mervin Sayese, to hear a man from our village tell Wetigo stories, which of course were in Cree. His name was Colin "Jackson" Cook. In my sister Anne Acco's book, *Ekosi: A Métisse Retrospective of Poetry and Prose*, she described him as being "a wizened little man whose anti-social behaviour made him the town boogeyman" (3).

Jackson's stories filled us with fear—the Wetigo was no ordinary monster. We were terrified, and then, just before dark, Jackson told us to go home. My home was the farthest away. As we tore down a narrow foot path, someone always tried to trip me from behind (the older boys enjoyed scaring us younger kids), and when I got tripped I wasted no time getting back on my feet.

The Wetigo (my phonetic version of the Swampy Cree Wītigō)—or Wīhtikow, Windigo, Wendigo among many other spellings in other languages—is a being common in traditional belief systems of many Indigenous North Americans, particularly Algonquin speakers, including the Ojibwe, Cree, Saulteaux, Naskapi, and Innu. I have read accounts of it in Samuel Hearne's journals from 1775, in David Thompson's journals from 1796 (Thompson refers to a Weetego), and in Louis Bird's book, *The Spirit Lives in the Mind: Omushkego Stories, Lives, and Dreams*, in which it is spelled Wihtigo. The early explorers described the Wetigo as a murderous, cannibalistic human. Bird, a member of the Winisk First Nation, explains that his version is a creature once human, either male or female, that has become possessed by a spirit whose main intent is to capture other humans for them to become assistant evildoers.

I dreaded the thought that my dad took me along on trips to fight that monstrous Wetigo. But after he and his friend chuckled at the idea, I thought maybe the Wetigo wasn't so scary after all. It was summer, and the Wetigo must have gone away, for often it is a creature of the cold or winter, associated with insatiable hunger or starvation. But I also felt that my father was not afraid of monsters, that he knew how to deal with them. However, I still faced my position with great apprehension and perhaps some wonder.

When I spoke with my brother Les about our dad being fearless, as he had made me believe while on a frightening boat trip with him on Namew Lake, which I will speak of in the next chapter, Les commented that our father, like all of the Cumberland House veterans of the two world wars, had lived through the most terrifying wars ever known, that the pain and suffering they had experienced were beyond belief. As a result, everything that nature now threw at them, even a Wetigo, seemed mild after the battlefields of Europe.

I remembered my mother's story of when my father was released from an army hospital in England. After he recovered enough from his war wounds to be moved, the Canadian army gave him an honourable discharge. He was sent home on a ship to the Halifax harbour and then took the long train ride to The Pas. My mother said that my dad's older brother Jonas took a small horse with an open carriole sled to pick him up. She said when Jonas met him at The Pas, he was shocked by my dad's physical appearance. His face was injured and had dropped on one side and was still bleeding, and Dad had covered it with a cloth to keep the bleeding down.

Jonas and my father started out on the trip from The Pas back to Cumberland House on a cold winter day. When my dad arrived home, many in the village could not stand looking at his appearance. My mother said that his own daughter, my oldest sister, Anne, was afraid of him, and it took her a while before she got used to having her father around. In fact, the children of Cumberland House would tease us Carriere children about my dad's disfigurement. My brother John recalls some cruel words said when we were growing up—some people called us "the twisted face children." I also heard "Kipāpā ana pīmitōn" ("Your dad is the one with a crooked mouth"). This was said to hurt my feelings, and as a child it bothered me, but it never hurt long because, when Dad was home, he would spend time with us in a warm and loving way. That really mattered. His love made those hateful and hurtful words go away.

Along with his physical discomforts and other health issues, my dad had to deal with what was known as "shell shock," what we know today as post-traumatic stress disorder or PTSD. It took him some time to recover. My brother John relayed a story told by both my aunts Elise and Marie Louise, who lived in the same neighbourhood as my parents. Some nights my father's sisters would see my dad running from house to house, crouching and calling out loud "I'm looking for Nazi German soldiers. They are here, somewhere!" Some called him ēgīskwēyāt (crazy) or said "Wīna mwātēs ēgīgwātagītāt" ("He was the one who suffered the most"). Later in this book, in the interviews with my aunts and other family members, they speak about my father's wartime experience and the physical and mental health problems that he had upon his return from overseas.

In the years that followed, my father never talked to us about his war experience, and what I learned came from others. I know that on August 23, 1944, he suffered a shrapnel injury from an explosive device while fighting on the front lines. It was a back injury, and in his top physical condition he was not deterred. He went back into battle after medical treatment. But Dad told his friend Ron Mackay that when he was injured during a firefight on the front lines on September 15, 1944, he knew his wound was serious but not enough to kill him right away. A bullet had entered his face, shattering his jaw bone, and continued through the back of his neck, just missing his vertebrae. He lay very still with his eyes closed so he would look dead to the enemy. The tactic worked, and the sniper then moved on without bothering to finish him off. My brother John told me that, according to my father's comrade Frank "Whitey" Chaboyer, also from Cumberland House and on the front lines at the time, Dad then passed out, and when the field staff arrived his head wound looked severe enough that they started to put him into a body bag. Frank told the field staff that his friend was still alive and, with the help of another comrade, Edward Fast from Nipawin, carried him to a Red Cross field hospital. Frank also said that Dad had reached the rank of a sergeant and had been in

My dad's army photo. Dad was a soldier in the Canadian Armed Forces in the Second World War.

Photo from the collection of Nora Agnes Carriere.

charge of a group of twenty soldiers on the front lines in German-occupied France. My father had enlisted in the Canadian army in January 1942, returned to Canada in January 1945, and was formally discharged from service on February 26 the same year. He lived in considerable pain most of his life afterward, but one wouldn't have known it. My mother often said "Ēgīmōtāpinēt" ("He is hiding his pain").

My brother Les said that, when Frank Chaboyer later came to visit Cumberland House, our parents gave him a celebration of the kind reserved for a returning war hero (which he was), and they named the first child born to them after Dad came home, a boy, Franklin in his honour.

Returning to their lives on their traplines was a welcome relief for our Indigenous war veterans. They had grown up living with Nature, and upon their return Nature was their relative, provider, and companion—in all respects, it was like a mother. The men's own mothers had been praying for their wayward sons to return from the war, and the lucky ones returned home not only to them but also to Mother Earth. But they were traumatized. So they embraced the bushland skills they had learned in their youth, and they took to their bush life with a spiritual awakening, Wetigos or not.

WETIGO RAISING HELL AND HIGH WATER

Wetigo has found the fossilized remains of the ancient Earth.
In buried basins at the heart and head of Turtle Island.
Wetigo will bring that buried fossil fuel to surface.
This will make money to feed hungry machines.
Wetigo can always buy time before digging.
Once dug up that fossil fuel will be in its hands.
Wetigo is sucking blood at the heart of Turtle Island.
Soon it will reach the arteries of Mother Earth.
Making them steam, gurgle, bulge and sputter.
Fed by pressurized water pumped down to her.
Mobile melted rock can move anywhere.
Following loosened arteries molten rock creeps up.
Once it finds a passage way to the surface.
It will drive the lava smashing through the upper Crust.
It may arrive at the surface like a ginormous solar flare.
Wetigo knows the inner workings of a magma chamber.
Endangering all the living creatures on Mother Earth.
Erupting volcanoes change everything right now.
Wetigo is sucking blood at the head of Turtle Island.
There are massive ice sheets on top of arctic oilfields.
Everything is full steam ahead to bring up the fossil fuel.
Opened ice flow lanes have ships carrying crude to market.
This will advance the melting of a continental ice sheet.
Wetigo saw coastal flooding and said, "too freaking bad!"
Wetigo tastes the future all we can tell is what it never had.
Its spirit screams, "Nobody can know when a volcano will blow!
Climate catastrophes come and go, so shut the hell up!"
Wetigo will stay this way until everything is gone.

When you idle so much, worries of Wetigo go on.
Take care of your health, your husky, your horse.
Then with your strength and good heart move on.

Written by Ken Carriere during a mild and cold October in 2018.

NO FEAR, STAY CALM

◇

One late-August day in 1961, when I was ten, my father and I travelled to Sturgeon Landing at the northeast end of Namew Lake, or Namēw Sākahigan as we call it, meaning Sturgeon Lake. It was a thirty-mile trip by boat from Cumberland House. My father drove a twenty-foot freighter canoe with a ten-horse-power outboard motor. This trip had three purposes. One was to bring my cousin Mildred Goulet, who had visited relatives in Cranberry Portage and The Pas for the summer, back to Cumberland. Another was to make a deal with a supplier of outboard motor fuel, Medric Poirier, before Dad started his fall guiding business. The third purpose was to meet with the Sturgeon Landing cooperative fishers' local leader, Charlie Budd. My dad was then the president of the Northern Saskatchewan Cooperative Fisheries producers.

I remember this trip to Sturgeon Landing well, for I was terrified as we travelled the full length of Namew Lake. The wind was from the northeast, a wind known as apisci kīwēcinōs (AK) by the Swampy Cree. Namew Lake is quite deep and stretches in a northeast direction. Since the

Charlie Budd from Sturgeon Landing on the shore of the Bigstone River. He was the leader of the commercial fishers at Namew Lake and a family friend.

Photo courtesy of Franklin Carriere of La Ronge, Saskatchewan.

northeast wind was in full force during our crossing, the waves reached their top height. In this country, there are two winds that concern the Cree: the kīwētin or K (north wind) and the apisci-kīwēcinōs or AK (little north wind), directionally the northeast wind. Even though the AK wind is a diminutive of the K wind, it still packs a mean punch.

We drove into waves that were so high that the freighter had to climb each swell before cresting the wave, and then we drove down the length on the downward slope. The distance between each crest stretched wide. I recall that the twenty-foot canoe was only about a quarter of the length between each crest.

Seated at the front, I was looking down at the water as we drove into each wave trough, and I was terrified at seeing the lake water rushing toward the bow. On the upward slope, I was looking at the sky filled with floating clouds. After going over several waves and getting cold spray in my face, I decided to turn around and cover up under a canvas tarp to avoid seeing the water rise and fall. I watched my father as he navigated the freighter canoe across the deepest parts of the lake. He looked so calm except for when the odd cold splash caught him. Now and then he would reach for his bailing bucket and calmly bail water out of the freighter as he held one hand firmly on the steering bar of the outboard motor. We drove along the lake's western shore close to its rocky outcroppings, and the huge waves smashed onto the rocks and sent their spray high into the forest cover. I could see that there was no place to beach the canoe, nowhere to take a break from the treacherous waves. We had to keep going no matter what came our way.

Finally, we got to Sturgeon Landing, where I had the pleasure of viewing the Sturgeon-weir River as it emptied out into Namew Lake. The river was roaring rapids with clear blue water, which we describe in Cree as wāsēyāgamin. Seeing clear water was a rare experience for me.

As I mentioned, I grew up at Kāministikominahikoskāk (Spruce Island, or Cumberland Island, as we sometimes call it). The island is bounded by Cumberland Lake on the north, the Bigstone River on the west, the Tearing River on the east, and the Saskatchewan River on the south. Cumberland Lake carries soil, silt, and soft clay; the Bigstone River is a meandering river with fine silt beds; and the Tearing River is a series of river channels with a gravel, silt, and clay mix base and a series of small rapids. (In Cree, we call the Tearing River Kāsīpāskāsik, meaning where the water seeps underground.) The Saskatchewan River also carries a load of silt, clay, and fine sand. (We describe muddy or silt-loaded water as asiskiyāgamin.) So the only time I saw any clear water, or wāsēyāgamin, while growing up was when we paddled just south of Budd's Point, where the clear blue water that flows from Namew Lake down the Sturgeon-weir enters the southeast end of Cumberland Lake.

At Sturgeon Landing, my cousin Mildred and I waited by the rapids near Medric Poirier's store while my father finished his business dealings. In the late afternoon, we travelled back home to Cumberland House. The wind had begun to die down, so we took a direct route across the lake instead of along the shoreline, and thankfully the trip was peaceful.

Medric Poirier and his helper poling to get past the last rapids just below Cumberland Lake, visible at the top of the photo, as his barge goes upstream on the Tearing River in 1951. They had picked up groceries, freight, gasoline, and diesel at The Pas and were on their way back to Sturgeon Landing.

Photo by Don Neilson, from the Ron Mackay Collection, Northern Saskatchewan Archives, La Ronge, Saskatchewan.

The sky was blue, filled with fluffy clouds that in my young imagination were animal features and people's faces.

When we got home, I told my frightening account of our outbound trip to my mother. She said that Namew Lake had a reputation for claiming the lives of lake travellers and that that summer alone two people had drowned there. My mother had grown up farther north along the Sturgeon-weir, at Āmisko Sākahigan (Amisk or Beaver Lake), and she was familiar with lake travel on both Namew and Amisk Lakes. In the days before Cumberland Lake began silting in because of the upstream dams and became shallower, it, too, had been a deep enough and treacherous lake.

One of my mother's stories relates to her experiences as a child growing up in this country.

Nigāwī ōma otayācimowin ēyācimāt otāwīpana. Ēkospīk nāntaw mitahāt pēyakosāp itātwāw askīnēt. (This is my mother's story as she told about her late father. She was about eleven years old at that time.)

KAMĀMAWI NISTĀPĀWANAW (WE WILL DROWN TOGETHER)

Tāpwē māga kāgīmosōmiyan,

This is true about your late grandfather,

mīna mīcētwāw nimāmitonēnimāw

and I often think about

tāgīsigaskītāt.

the things he was able to do.

Nigīpēyakwopigīgonān tāgotāwiyāk.

My late father raised us by himself.

Osāmiwīpac ēgīnagataskwēt tāgogāwiyāk.

My late mother died too soon.

Tāgotāwiyāk kīnōtāwi osīcigēw,

My late father knew how to make things,

kīnōtāwi pāgwēsiganīgēw,

he could bake bannock,

kīnagacīsiw.

he was good at everything.

Ēgosītāt mistikocīmana,

He made wooden skiffs,

ēgīpimastāt sāgahiganihk,

he sailed them on the lake,

asici kīpimipanītwāw piyāpiskos.

he also drove a small motor.

Ēgwāni kāmisagāyāk

When we arrived on shore

sēmāk gīkotawēw,

he made a campfire right away,

gīpāgwēsiganīgēw gotawānihk.

he made bannock over the campfire.

Namwāc wīgāc nigīgisisīpīgiskwātigonān.

He never spoke in anger to us.

Nigīminopamīgonān.

He took good care of us.

Kiyām ātawina ēgīpēyakopigīgoyāk.	*Even though he was alone* *raising us.*
Êgwāni ēgwaspīk ēpimōtēwāk	*This time as we were travelling*
Amisko sāgahiganihk	*on Amisk (Beaver) Lake*
mēgwāc ētiyāgatīk.	*while it was freezing over.*
Kīgīstinīpaniw.	*It got very windy.*
Kīsōgāgamāskāw.	*The waves were powerful.*
Nigīsēgisinān nīyanān awasisak.	*We were scared, us children.*
Naganipitigonān mistipāgwāson.	*He covered us with a big canvas tarp.*
Mitoni ēmaskamīpanik	*The water just iced up*
nipī kāpōsāstāk.	*as it dropped inside the boat.*
Êgota tāgītigoyāk kimosōmpan,	*This is what your late grandfather* *said to us,*
"Kīspin kigatapāwgonaw,	*"If our boat capsizes,*
ātawina kamāmawi nistāpawānaw."	*it will not matter since we will drown* *together."*

Written in January 1993, as told to Ken Carriere by his mother, Agnes Carriere. The story is about her late father, Dougal McKenzie, and recounts events of November 1926 on Amisk Lake in northeastern Saskatchewan.

My maternal grandfather, Dougal McKenzie, and his family at their home on the Amisk Lake Indian Reserve in Saskatchewan, 1933. From right to left: Dougal, Christiana Cursiteur (Dougal's second wife) holding baby Elizabeth, Katherine, my mother Agnes with toddler Murdoch standing in front of her, Donald, Lily, Josephine, and Ethel. Elizabeth and Murdoch were born to Dougal and Christiana; the other children were offspring of Dougal's first wife, Virginie Jourdain.

Photo courtesy of the Provincial Archives of Saskatchewan, S-B9788.

CHEECHIGANIHK AND THE BIG BEND

◇

n 1964, when I was thirteen, my father and I travelled into the heart of the Upper Delta during the summer commercial fishing season. Our destination was on the Central Angling River, a place called Cheechiganihk (Cheechigan's Place), on David Goulet's trapline. David was my father's friend, the one with whom Dad had joked a couple of years earlier that I was the one to strike the Wetigo.

When we left home, we walked down to the Bigstone River landing. There was only one main road for vehicles, a few horse-drawn wagon trails, and many footpaths. My family had no vehicle. My mother had prepared a small bag of groceries, freshly made bannock, and some dried moose meat (nīwayiganak) mixed with tallow and raisins. We took enough grub for supper and for breakfast and lunch the next day. All our equipment was stored inside a locked shed at the Bigstone River landing, where arrangements were made for a plane to fly in from Amisk Lake to pick up fish for transport to the fish plant at Denare Beach. We picked up sold blocks of ice at the icehouse behind the fish weigh station and storage unit. Then we loaded our grub box (mīcisowini mistigawat),

My grandfather Dougal McKenzie, a riverboat deckhand, is shown at the front of the lower deck, at right, wearing a tie, with his hands on his hips. His son Bill ("Steamboat Bill") also worked on the steamboat, as did Chief Tom Settee of the Cumberland Band. One reason these men did this work was that they knew the river channels very well.

Photo courtesy of Nora Agnes Carriere.

a ten-gallon barrel (mākākos) of gasoline (pimiy), some out-board motor oil for mixing with the gas, a gasoline tank with mixed gas for the ten-horsepower Johnson outboard motor (in our Cree, it is called pīwāpisk), extra wooden fish boxes, ice blocks covered with a wetted burlap bag, and a canvas tarp, and we set off for Cheechiganihk.

We went down the full length of the Bigstone River, then turned southwest at the Cutoff to head upstream (natimihk) on the New Channel of the Saskatchewan River. Then we motored on by the southwestern shore of Cumberland Lake past two small islands (ministikwāpiskosa or rocky islands). We saw other fishermen camped on these islands, and their nets were already set. We went by a place called Alum Bay. We continued on toward a point of land on the western shore of Pine Island, a place called Dinner Point. During the days when they ran steamboats on Cumberland Lake, they moored there to provide their passengers with dinner or lunch, hence the name. It was also there that canoe travellers going upstream stopped for lunch or dinner. South of Dinner Point, we passed a place called Kāgaskitēwi Askīyogāhk (Black Mud Bay), which lies on the most southwesterly shore of Cumberland Lake and stretches far inland to where it meets a stand of aspen and maple trees.

Once we got past Dinner Point, we entered the Central Angling River, a wide river, and we followed it until it became a river of medium width, with a shoreline of mixed growth of willow and tall aspen poplar. We came to a place where the river flows beside a lake to the west. This lake was called the Sturgeon Fisheries. We continued our trip onto a wide and straight-flowing river with mature growth of tall aspen forest on both sides. We were getting closer to the big bend of the Central Angling, where we would set our nets. When we reached Cheechiganihk, we had been travelling for three hours from the time we left the Bigstone River landing fish station.

Cheechiganihk was at a big bend of the Central Angling River by the South Angling River junction. It appears that the South Angling was there before the Central Angling. If you were to study it carefully, you might surmise that the bend is there because the intrusion of the South Angling made it. This area was an excellent fishing spot. The South Angling straddled Dumbell Lake to the south, and to its west was Muskeg Lake. Out of Muskeg Lake flowed a small waterway called Gun Creek, which got its name from a musket dropped into the water by a Cree hunter during the early fur trade era. He had shot a moose from his canoe, which tipped over from the recoil of the exploding gunpowder. In Cree, we call the spot pāskisigan agōtin, the place where a gun is under water. My brother John found the musket at a point off the South Angling.

When we got to our campsite, we unloaded the block of ice that we had stored inside a wooden fish box and covered it with a wetted canvas tarp since it gets very hot during the day in late July and early August. My father had the locations picked out for setting our nets. Often these choices were routine—usually, it was one net for the entrance to Dumbell Lake beside the South Angling and another one along the South Angling—but sometimes he wanted to try new sites with a single net at each location.

At the big bend, we set two small mesh nets for goldeye, sauger, and pickerel. We set two more small mesh nets at the rivulets that flowed out of Muskeg Lake into the Central Angling. At the junction of the South Angling and the Central Angling, we set a ten-and-a-half-inch mesh gill net for catching sturgeon.

My dad set up a campsite with a large canvas tent (pagwānigamik) where we would stay overnight. In the evening after supper, before it got dark, we checked our nets. Whatever we caught then was gutted and put into our wooden fish boxes and covered with ice chips. We would get up early in the morning to check the nets again and pull them out.

At all locations connected with the Central Angling we pulled in a good catch of goldeye, pickerel, and sauger. At the South Angling location beside Dumbell Lake, we caught a few pickerel (ogāwak), sauger (ogāsak), goldeye (wīpicīsak), and pike (wīcēgāpīs), at that time a low-priced commercial fish. The locations where the rivulets flow from Muskeg Lake into the Central Angling had the finest commercial fish found anywhere. On average, the pickerel and sauger were about four pounds per fish, the goldeye about two and a half pounds. My dad's smile told me he liked it there. The bears didn't even seem to bother him.

I remember one time when we were at Cheechiganihk Dad took a nap after breakfast. He had finished dressing the fish and iced them, and our fish-filled boxes sat in the long shadows of the shoreline. I was playing in the sandbar of the big bend when I heard a noise like someone hitting the side of the tent, a grunting noise, and then a shuffling off into the willow bushes. I went cautiously to check what had just made the noises, but Dad was still inside the tent and snoring. I saw fresh paw prints on the sand close to the tent. A bear had come to visit the camp and had come very close to where my father was resting. Dad must have sensed it and hit the side of the tent to scare it off and gone right back to sleep after he scared the bear away. When he got up, he lit a cigarette and had a cup of coffee.

When we camped overnight, we checked the nets early each morning. We'd pull in a few more loads of fish and take each net out after removing them. My dad used a kēcigwāskwocigan (fish-removing net hook), a bent nail with a filed tip placed on a wooden handle wrapped with fishing twine and then soaked with an ambroid paste for a waterproof finish. He'd work quickly with the net hook to make sure the catch was kept fresh.

Back at the campsite, he would dress the fish and place them inside the wooden fish boxes with ice chips to keep them cool. While he was busy getting the fish ready, I had the chore of hanging the fishnets up to clean and dry. This task is called mīnostaginigē (straightening out the net for resetting). I would hang the nets up on two poles—one side had the corks or floats and the other side the leads or weights. The floats and weights are placed opposite to each other on the gillnets. They were hooked onto the drying poles. I'd then join my dad to learn how to clean and dress the fish so we could get done quicker. The sun would already be starting to heat things up, so we needed to ensure that our catch would not spoil. We left at about 9:00 a.m., and our trip downstream to the fish station and then back home took about the same amount of time as when we came upstream without a load—approximately three hours. At Bigstone River landing, there was a small shack where we weighed the fish and then placed them with ice in wooden boxes for shipment.

After completing this work, we'd go home to a full meal prepared by my mom. We had fresh bannock, moose meat with potatoes, carrots, and onions—all veggies from her garden. Dad would rest for a while, and I'd go outside to play with my younger brother Clifford. Around 3:00 p.m. the same day, we'd head out for another trip to Cheechiganihk. We would arrive by 6:00 p.m., set the nets, check ones we had left set up before dark, camp overnight, and check our nets again in the morning. We would repeat this routine like clockwork for a week or two.

MUSKRATS AT SALT LAKE

◇

nother adventure I remember was during the 1964 spring muskrat-trapping season, when I was on Easter break from school. We left our home in early April for Salt Lake, in the northeastern part of an area known as the Hudson's Bay Company Fur Lease. This was an area roughly between the Manitoba border on the east, the Dragline Channel on the west (created using a dragline excavator), the Old Channel of the Saskatchewan River on the north, and the Birch River on the south. It was an area of roughly 320,000 acres that the Hudson's Bay Company leased from Saskatchewan from the 1930s to the mid-1960s because of its interest in muskrat pelt production. We travelled to Salt Lake by dog team on the Saskatchewan River to Acāpāskonigāpihk (in English called Willow Portage) and then went southeast until we got to our trapping area.

It is worth noting that the two lakes we traversed on this trip—known to us as Willow Lake, accessed via Willow Portage, and Salt Lake—appear on modern maps as the McGregor Lakes. In 1947, the government of Saskatchewan began naming, and renaming, geographic features in the province's north after servicemen who had been killed in the Second World War and the Korean War, and what we still know locally as Willow and Salt Lakes were, unknown to us, renamed in honour of Alexander and David McGregor, two young men from Regina who sadly had lost their lives in the earlier conflict. In fact, however noble an initiative the "geomemorial" project seemed to be, many places long known by Indigenous names were given new appellations under this scheme.

At Salt Lake, or the southeastern shore of what are also known as the two McGregor Lakes, we joined a group of trappers from Cumberland House and Pemmican Portage. They had set up their camps on a height of land that had a fair amount of firewood and an open creek where we could get drinking water. My brother Franklin was nineteen years old and a skilled trapper, hunter, fisher, and overall bushman by then. He had gone ahead with his dog team to the trapping area. He picked the spot to camp and set up the prospector tent in which all three of us would stay. Dad showed me how to make a bed of logs like a crib above the ground and to gather hay for a mattress. Once I had made my bed and spread out my feather blanket, it was my job to gather firewood and melt snow for washing and making tea. Dad had used five dogs for the trip, and I had ridden in the sleigh with him. This type of sleigh was called a jumper sled, and the load on it had included a sixteen-foot canoe, paddles, stop-loss traps, guns, blankets, changes of clothes, a grub box, and other camp items.

The other families already set up and trapping in the surrounding area told us what was still open, and that became our trapping area. The women and their daughters present were the skinners, and they were paid an agreed-upon amount for the skinning. Their job was to remove the fur pelts from the muskrat carcasses. They would then stretch them over two strips of boards. These stretchers were adjustable at one end to enable them to fit different sizes of pelts.

The muskrat carcasses were kept for meat consumption and smoked dry over a campfire to preserve them, and whatever was not eaten was taken back home after the trapping was done.

The muskrat meat was the main source of protein for the trappers and their families at the trapping area, and the women cooked a good supply to feed everyone. At different times, someone would bring over a cooking pot full of smoked muskrat meat and potatoes along with fresh bannock. At this camp, all we had to do was boil water for cleaning and making tea. My dad had a trapping area with willow bluffs and small bays. I went with him on the jumper sled. We went about setting the stop-loss traps inside the "rat" houses. The snow was melting fast, and in a short while the sun was hanging at mid-arch for up to four hours and lighting the sky for up to fourteen hours a day. Salt Lake was in a condition called ēwānitoskopēyāk, which in Cree means the lake ice is melting along the shoreline.

With the ice melting along the lake's edges, we started using our canoe and went about setting traps on push-ups— structures muskrats build of mud and vegetation in the winter over a hole in the ice and that are insulated and safe from predators, where the animals can come up for a breath, to feed, or to rest. Unlike beavers, which cache their food for the winter, muskrats are active throughout it, having to forage continually. In my opinion, muskrats are the busiest of all the water-dwelling creatures, a close match to the beaver. The only thing that slows a muskrat down is the number of predators that would take its life.

With the weather warming, the muskrats were no longer confined to their lodges and were starting to venture out. As the spring progressed, however, they began fighting with one another over potential mates and territory, behaviour that Cree trappers call ēpīgamitocik, meaning they are cutting each other with their sharp teeth. Many would be injured, some dying from their wounds. So it was time to

Two families spring muskrat trapping in an area known as Morganihk (Morgan's Place), located upstream from Cumberland House between the Old and New Channels of the Saskatchewan River. My brother John said it was a habitat where muskrats thrived. The people in the photo, from left to right, are George "Fisher" McAuley Sr., Rosalie McAuley, Virginia (Ischiny) Morin, with grandson Ronnie Morin in front of her, and my great-uncle Joe Morin. Rosalie and Virginia are the daughters of Solomon Carriere and his wife, Marie McKay, my father's uncle and aunt. The proudly displayed snowshoes were handmade by Joe Morin.

Photo courtesy of Virginia Janet Forest of the Nemeiben River Reserve (formerly the Sucker River First Nation), Lac La Ronge Indian Band.

stop trapping muskrats, leave the marshes, and head home, for the pelts would be torn—a skinner would need surgical tools to stitch together the cut hides, requiring extra work.

Our trip back to Cumberland House presented a challenge. We needed to find an alternative route since the Saskatchewan River ice was opening up along the shoreline because of the fast current. The Cree had named this river Kiskāciwan for that fast current. I did not understand the meaning of this name while growing up since I stayed on the lake, or north, side of Spruce or Cumberland Island. I had only heard of our southern, riverside neighbour at Pemmican Portage as being called Kiskāciwanohk (The Place of the Fast River Current).

Initially, we took a winter road built for a Bombardier snow tracker that had a hard pack of snow and was shaded by white spruce and thick stands of Manitoba maple. We drove the dog team to the fur lease headquarters first to drop off our pelts and to collect the pay for them, and then we drove our team across the Saskatchewan River at a safe crossing and went home along a horse and wagon trail that still had a snow pack. But some parts of the trail had exposed ground, so we jumped off the jumper sled at times so the dogs didn't have to pull so hard. We would jump back on as soon as we were back on the snow pack. As always, the dogs seemed to know they were going home, so they were pulling hard and running fast.

CUT BEAVER LAKE

$\diamond$

n early August 1966, my father, his brother James, James's business partner Jean Baptiste Laliberte, and I travelled to Cut Beaver Lake for a commercial fishing venture. We used an eighteen-foot freighter canoe and a ten-horse-power Johnson outboard motor. There was a good steady flow of Rocky Mountain meltwater coming down from both the North Saskatchewan and South Saskatchewan Rivers. We left Cumberland House from the Bigstone River, went east over the Cut-Off Rapids, and then turned west to head upstream on the Old Channel of the Saskatchewan River. When we arrived at the Dragline Channel locking gate, we made a portage over the water-control structure that was placed there not only to allow both water and fish to enter the Cumberland Marshes via Cut Beaver River and Cut Beaver Lake but also to ensure that flooding did not happen farther downstream in Manitoba. We travelled down the Dragline Channel, which flowed southeastward into Cut Beaver Lake. This lake was shallow, but since there was a steady supply of water from the Old Channel it was at a good level for setting gillnets.

Baptiste, to those who knew him, was a powerful paddler. Along with his paddling partner Marcel (Oscigwān) Stewart, he had won the Flin Flon Gold Rush canoe derby in Manitoba more than once. Baptiste's other marathon canoe racing paddling partners included my uncle Roger Carriere as well as Joe Michel and Gib McAcheran. Baptiste had even raced in international competition with my uncle Roger at *La classique internationale de canots de la Mauricie*, held every year at Shawinigan, Quebec, since 1934. When I was fifteen, I had the privilege of canoeing the freighter with Baptiste when he went out to hunt ducks on Cut Beaver Lake. When he chased down a group of canvasback ducks, the bow of the freighter almost lifted off the water. His powerful strokes enabled us to get close enough for him to shoot the ducks as they desperately tried to swim away from us.

At Cut Beaver Lake, we fished for whitefish, pickerel, pike, sauger, and goldeye using small (four-and-a-half-inch) mesh gillnets. All these species were a good meat source, and there was a market for them in Winnipeg and the Midwestern United States. At this time, in 1966, it was still about a year before an all-weather road was built connecting Cumberland House to the world beyond, so as I mentioned earlier our fish had to be flown from Bigstone River landing to the Amisk Lake fish plant at Denare Beach. From there, they were taken to Flin Flon and loaded onto a refrigerated railcar and shipped to Winnipeg.

One of the bush plane pilots we got to know over the years was a man named Ed LeClair, who flew a Cessna 185 float plane. He would bring in gasoline and groceries as well as ice blocks and fish boxes from the fish plant at Amisk Lake. I was amazed at how Ed flew that plane. He would land out on the lake at first to get his bearings; after that, he would land right on the river channel close to the loading dock. At this point, the river's width was only about three times that of the plane's wing span.

At this time, there was a provincial government fisheries biologist named Leroy Royer and an assistant at the Bigstone River fish station. Among other things, they were studying the species of mooneye and goldeye that swam together, being particularly interested in the number of mooneye. I was shown the difference between the two fish; it was not much except for the colour of the eye. The biologists also studied what the fish ate. I learned that they would eat small minnows, fish flies, and even mice and that they had a great number of small teeth that not only came out of their jaws but were also on their tongues, which is why the Cree call them wīpicīsisak (meaning fish with the small teeth).

MOSSY RIVER CAMP

———————⬦———————

n the 1960s, my father operated a hunting and fishing lodge on the Mossy River, where he would also fish for sturgeon to sell commercially. My parents would take us children to the lodge in August to help get the place ready for the fall season, when the hunters would come, from early September to late October, before freeze-up (kāmigiskāk). But our parents also took us there to experience the wilderness.

To them, the camp at Mossy River was like a homecoming; I could tell by the stories they shared with each other. They talked about the people who made a living in this area, the familiar small lakes and creeks (sākahiganisa ekwa sīpīsisa) and animals (pisiskiwak). Listening to them, I thought they were sharing happy and unforgettable memories. My mother, being very spiritual, would say "Ninanāskomāw kimanitōminaw kīpyapic kitaskīnaw ēminwāsik" ("I thank our Creator that our land is still good"). My father would nod his head in approval. My mother had said the thanksgiving for us to hear.

My mother with her younger sister Josephine beside their trapping cabin at Bear's Head by the Mossy River trapping area.

Photo by Dougal McKenzie, archived by my aunts, Kate Dubinak of Creighton, Saskatchewan, and Josephine Carriere of Cumberland House, Saskatchewan.

My father had taken my mother to this place after marrying her. He had grown up nearby at the Pine Bluff Indian Reserve; she had grown up somewhat to the north on the Amisk Lake Indian Reserve. They both knew how to live off the land. Together they had run a trapline on the upper Mossy River along with my mother's in-laws and her younger sisters Josephine and Ethel. And before my father went to war, he and my mother also did spring trapping at Maskwostigwānīk (Bear's Head) on the southern shore of the Mossy River at a point off Pine Island.

When I think of it now, the camp by the Mossy River reminds me of the movie *Jurassic Park*. Sitting on top of the lower Paleozoic limestone bedrock, it is a predator-prey, wide-open zoo. Wolves eat moose, snakes eat mice and frogs, fish eat snakes, and so on. My mom was quite afraid of wolves ever since she had witnessed from her cabin a sled dog being attacked and killed by a wolf.

Part of getting the Mossy River camp prepared for the fall hunters was attending to the grounds and buildings, which always needed maintenance. We would cut the long grasses and sedges that had grown to form a thick and tall hay meadow, using a long scythe, grass whips, rakes, and a push lawn mower. In no time, we had a small haystack that we would burn in the early evening to make a smoke smudge before fogs of mosquitoes drifted our way. Once we had the yard taken care of, a woodpile stacked, outhouses cleaned, and the cook shack readied, where meals would be prepared and people could eat and visit, all was good.

My dad said that, when he first started the outfitting business, he had two buildings. One was the cook shack, the other a cabin for the tourists. The guides slept in tents on a tarp spread out on the ground, but after two or three seasons my father built another cabin for their sleeping quarters.

In August 1967, on our second day at the camp that year, I remember that my father started fishing. He set a fifty-yard gillnet for catching pickerel, goldeye, and lake suckers for our food. The suckers Mom would smoke and dry. In the early morning, Dad set a gillnet at the mouth of a small river that branched west on the Mossy River just downstream from the lodge, and soon he had enough fish to feed us for two days. With a good supply of lake suckers, he cut some into cubes to attach to a line of hooks as bait for catching sturgeon. But besides using lines with hooks, he used gillnets for catching sturgeon, which is where I came in. I had become the outboard motor operator for my dad by this time, but I was not prepared for the task he set for me then.

Dad sat at the bow of the canoe with a sturgeon net and told me to drive to the north side of Mossy River, then to run the motor in reverse as he lowered the net into the water. He made sure that the weights and the floats on either side of the net were kept parallel to one another and that the net didn't cross over them. Sometimes I ran the motor too fast, though, leaving him struggling and hanging on to the net before pulling it closer to the south shore. The proper place to put this type of floating net was at midstream.

Dad managed to get the net laid out, but it was bunched up in some spots, so our next manoeuvre was to go back to the north shore to pull the net back from there. This required me to drive up to the net, stop, and—while he grabbed the net—put the engine in reverse. I wasn't such an accomplished motor operator, and my dad got frustrated as he tried to straighten the net out while we were floating downstream with it. When setting a gillnet, you try to keep it straight, which in Cree is called ēkawēsk agōcigēyan. But, unfortunately, our attempts to do this, with a motor continuously running back and forth near the net, didn't result in our catching any sturgeon that day.

My brother John told me that the technique we tried is called ēcīmawāt anapiya (floating a net with a canoe as you go downstream with it). Another method we could have used was to float a net downstream in a U shape. This method can raise the chances of getting a fish caught in the net, which in

Cree is called agawāpago. While sturgeon fishing specifically, it is known as ēgawāpawāt namēwa (he is corralling the sturgeon into the net). This technique is also known as seining. When my father was younger, he had used this method of sturgeon "corralling" before they had outboard motors; more than likely, it required two canoes to keep the net U shaped.

My brother John also told me that sturgeon fishing was done on both the upper and lower Mossy River for a very long time and that, before ice houses were used, fishers kept their sturgeon in shallow pools on the ministikwāpiskwa (rocky islands) in Cumberland Lake. These pools were at lake level with small openings between the limestone rock slabs that allowed fresh water, minnows, and crustaceans to enter. The sturgeon could feed and were kept in the pools until someone came along to purchase them. Fishers now keep sturgeon in the water using a tether line run through their gills and down through their mouths. This allows the fish to continue to catch food while secured. Fishers usually pick a spot beside a thick underbrush of willows so the line isn't easy to see, not marking the spot but memorizing it. With a tether, a sturgeon could be kept in the water for at least one week, for the goal was to catch a certain number before taking them to market. Once a fisher had his catch, and the lines of hooks and the gillnets were pulled out, the fish were taken home to be weighed and prepared for shipping. In addition to the Amisk Lake fish plant at Denare Beach, my brother John told me, at one time there were fish plants in The Pas, and the fish market was in Winnipeg. Both Booth Fisheries and Co-op Fisheries had fish plants at The Pas. The famous Booth Fisheries was an American-based company that had established itself in Manitoba in the 1880s and had dominated commercial fishing for decades. Nowadays, all commercially caught fish in northern Saskatchewan and Manitoba must be sold to the Freshwater Fish Marketing Corporation, whose head office is in Winnipeg and whose markets are now global.

The Booth Fisheries barge from The Pas on the Saskatchewan River, moored at Kiskáciwanohk (or Pemmican Portage), circa early 1950s. It arrived once a week with fresh produce, supplies, and mail, and local people called it the "banana boat" because the only time we had bananas was when this barge arrived.

Photo from the Ron Mackay Collection, Northern Saskatchewan Archives, La Ronge, Saskatchewan.

In the time our family was at the Mossy River outfitting camp that August of 1967, my dad caught four sturgeon to take to market in spite of my failure as an outboard motor operator. He caught them on two separate lines of fishhooks. He set a sturgeon net at the mouth of the Windy Lake out-let stream into the Mossy River where an eddy had formed, but did not catch any large, sellable sturgeon there; instead, he caught some huge northern pike and a smaller sturgeon, which became our meals. When Mom prepared pike, or pickerel, she usually fried fillets with onions in a skillet and served them up with boiled potatoes and carrots from our garden back in Cumberland; the sturgeon was cut into steak sizes, boiled, and served with the vegetables. These meals

My father, Pierre Carriere, in the fall of 1969, when he was the owner of two outfitting camps for hunters.

*Photo courtesy of John Carriere, from Dick Flood's photos in my sister Donna
Mirasty's collection.*

were favourites, leaving us so full we would need to rest or
nap a while to digest them. Then the energy would kick in
and get us going again to continue with our chores. The stay
at the camp was a busy one, but we enjoyed the wilderness
and spending the time with our parents. However, environ-
mental changes to Nitaskīnan, or Our Land, on the upper
Saskatchewan River Delta were upon us. From then on, the
summers of camp life by the Mossy River would change dra-
matically from year to year.

DO YOU FEEL THE SPIRIT OF A MOOSE?

———◇———

n the summer of 1963, when I was twelve years old, we experienced a big flood after the Squaw Rapids (E.B. Campbell) hydro dam was completed and the spillway was opened. The Bigstone River overflowed its banks, flooding Cumberland Island, and there were high water levels throughout much of the Saskatchewan River Delta. I saw the extent of the dam's impact when I had the chance to go on a long canoe trip with my dad's uncle Albert Flett, whom we called Ānipats. Ānipats worked for my father, mostly from August to October, taking care of his working dogs on Limestone Island, near a place called Snake Point on the west end of Cumberland Lake by Pine Island. We also knew Snake Point as Ānipacihk or Ānipats' (or Albert's) Place. It was where Ānipats had a trapper's cabin and a summer camping spot for tents. He always came to our house when Dad was home, and I was eager to go on this canoe trip with him.

For this trip, my mother gave us her blessing since she trusted Albert to keep me from drowning, although I was a good swimmer by twelve years old. I had started swimming when I was four or five along the shoreline of Cumberland

Lake and had nearly drowned several times, so I knew not to panic.

I helped Albert take his belongings from another cabin he had at the edge of our settlement down to the Bigstone River landing. He had a cast iron wheel attached to a wooden frame for a wheelbarrow, and everything that he needed for the trip fit onto its flat bed, so it took only a single trip.

We paddled out onto Cumberland Lake with no hesitation, but with the high water we stuck close to the shoreline as we paddled for one of the three islands just north of what we called Farm Island, where some farmers raised cattle and harvested oats, barley, and hay. When we got to the most northerly island, Albert stopped to boil water for tea, and he warmed up a pot of soup (sop) that he had prepared (ēgīsopīgēt) in the morning.

Later, when we arrived at Albert's summer camp, we found that it was under water, so Albert decided to go to Snake Point, on higher ground. As its name suggests, the place was crawling with garter snakes, which he tried to chase off with his paddle. But after we set up his tent, we found that some snakes had crawled under it for shade. His prospector tent had no floor cover, so the snakes had got in right away. That ended that, and we took the tent down and continued to paddle along the northeast shoreline of Pine Island toward Bear's Head, where, as I mentioned earlier, my mother and father had a trapline when they were younger. Albert located a dry camp spot that appealed to him, a spot we knew as Ēlin Cāwmasihk (Helen Thomas's place). Helen Thomas was my mother's stepmother's aunt.

We spent the first night sleeping in Albert's tent, which had holes in it big enough for raindrops to come through, but even worse they allowed mosquitoes inside. When we went to bed, Albert closed the tent flap, we ducked under sīsīp agōpa (duck down robes), and he took out a can of Flit with a pump attached to it and sprayed the inside of the tent with it. Flit was a chemical made to kill mosquitoes—and maybe people. Albert opened the tent flap to allow some mosquitoes to escape the killing fog, but many dropped dead before getting out. The Flit was so harsh it made me gag, and I covered my face to protect myself while I waited for the fog to clear. When I stuck my face out when I thought it was safe enough to breathe, I could hear so many mosquitoes buzzing outside the tent it was deafening. It seemed like a thundercloud of mosquitoes was trying to get inside the tent to torment us. This went on for quite a while. Many did make it inside the tent at first, but eventually the din of mosquito sounds died down as the air cooled. A few stragglers still managed to get in, but Albert then used the Flit sparingly to reduce their numbers.

After finally getting a good night's rest, we woke up the next morning shortly after daybreak. Albert made a campfire, boiled water for coffee, and fried up bacon with eggs. After breakfast, we took the tent down, packed everything back into the canoe, and continued on our trip. We paddled down the southwest side of Pine Island, but the water was so high, and the rivers we would normally follow were so flooded, that we needed to follow Albert's instincts about where to go.

Albert wanted to check out a place where he knew moose were often plentiful. I was at the bow of the canoe and on the watch for moose as we paddled slowly along trying not to make any noise, and Albert would whisper, "Kimacsōstawāw nā mōswa?" ("Do you sense the presence of a moose?"). His question surprised me. By "macsōstawāw," I thought he was asking if I had felt the spirit of a moose. Since I had been raised Roman Catholic with all its nuances, I wondered if the spirit of the moose was like the Holy Ghost, something mysterious. I began to wonder if the moose had a spirit or soul. Did the reference to a spirit mean that a ghost—a cīpay— was present? I tried to imagine what a ghost of a moose would look like. Maybe like a big horse wearing a white sheet with holes in it for its eyes. Like the horse that ran into my aunt Iskwēw's white bedsheet as it hung on the clothesline at night. Her neighbour, who saw the horse with the white sheet over it, was frightened beyond his wits, thinking he had seen a big scary ghost wandering the nearby meadow.

Perhaps in Albert's Cree worldview all animals have their own spirits, something academics call animism. In my worldview dominated by Christianity, I was uncertain of a spirituality in the animal world, but in many Indigenous cultures animals are the spirit helpers of humans. At home growing up, we were taught the principle of ocinēwin, which is not to practise excessive killing, or cause the unnecessary suffering, of animals. I carried this principle with me when I hunted rabbits. I checked my snares at regular times, and whenever a rabbit was still alive I would kill it quickly. Mom showed us how to do it. Sometimes, though, I could not bring myself to kill them, and instead I would bring them home to keep them as pets.

But Albert's question ("Kimacsōsatwāw nā mōswa?") really had less to do with animal spirits and more to do with observing any clues that animals might leave behind, traces of their physical presence that would give the hunter an idea about where they were and where they were going. The hunter has to know the moose's behaviour and habits. He has to understand the moose. One thing for sure is that moose can hear you from far away, so it is important to be quiet.

Albert showed me how to do a soundless paddle stroke, which requires bringing the paddle forward by turning it sideways and sliding it through the water without bringing it up. When you bring a paddle up from the water, you can make noise, and even a sprinkling of water on the surface can be loud enough for a moose to hear on a calm day. The type of stroke Albert taught me also makes it less likely that you'll bump the canoe with the paddle, another sound a moose could hear. Whenever I use that paddle stroke, the song my paddle sings is a lullaby.

We did this type of "soundless" paddling for a long stretch along the lakeshore, and according to Albert we were canoeing over flooded moose pastures. There were open spaces surrounded by willow bluffs and clumps of tall phragmites (astāganaskwak). The water was high, and we moved through the area quickly. We did not see any moose. We came to a place on the eastern edge of a large lake that was known as the Sturgeon Fisheries and paddled upstream to reach a height of land where a cabin called Whiteman's Shack stood on the eastern shore of the Central Angling River. Albert had hoped to stay at this cabin, but the floor was submerged by the floodwater. We kept paddling downstream on the Central Angling until we finally found high ground not flooded and came to a place that Albert liked. All during the trip, it was pouring rain. We set up camp and prepared supper, and at least with the downpour the mosquitoes were not such a nuisance. Keeping dry inside the holey tent was a problem, though, but having paddled all day we were tired and managed to get rest after all. The next morning we were greeted by a sunny day, had breakfast, and paddled home.

LITTLE CUMBERLAND

—◇—

n 1962, when I was eleven years old, I travelled with my dad to a place known to us Cumberland House Cree as Nistam Pawistik (or the First Rapids), a place named Squaw Rapids by non-Indigenous mapmakers. A temporary camp had been established there, a base for workers building the dam and hydroelectric power station that would have a great impact on the delta in the years to come. We called this work camp Little Cumberland because of the number of people from our community working there.

We left Cumberland House using a twenty-foot freighter canoe outfitted with a ten-horsepower Johnson outboard motor. The freighter had been re-ribbed with new cedar, had a fresh canvas outer shell painted with a linseed oil base, and had a fresh grass-green marine paint for a top coat, work my dad had hired his cousin Joe Dorion to do.

On the first day, we went as far as the Big Eddy outfitting camp, about fifty kilometres upstream on the Saskatchewan River. My dad and his brothers James and William had shares in this business. We stayed overnight, and the next morning we continued on upstream to Little Cumberland.

This part of the Saskatchewan River had a set of rapids that ran over mostly well-rounded glacial till boulders with no bedrock. The water was clear, and you could see the boulders as you passed over them. Dad drove straight into the rapids with no hesitation, navigating them easily. At our destination, he drove the freighter onto the shore just below the site where the hydroelectric power plant was under construction. Today a provincial recreation site is located there, across from the Thunder Rapids Lodge, which offers guiding services for hunting and fishing. We'd come to Little Cumberland to visit with relatives; my dad wanted to check, in particular, how my older brothers John and Franklin were doing as employees working on the project.

We walked up a very steep bank to reach the log cabins where our relatives were staying, and while Dad went about his meetings I found other children to play with. The whole place looked like a kind of junk yard, full of metal and wood, mostly construction or industrial grade, and with so much building material lying about it was an unusual place to play. A vivid memory that I have is that among the junk piles I came too close to a wasp nest and was stung on my forehead and was in great pain in an instant. Fortunately, the women from Little Cumberland treated me with some kind of a broadleaf plant and a face towel soaked in cold water that eventually took away the pain, but it also helped to hear the laughter of the women as they went about their daily chores.

Leaving this gigantic industrial site with all its commotion and going back downstream to the Big Eddy camp area was like waking up from a nightmare. The next year the "Squaw Rapids Dam" was commissioned; its name was changed to the E.B. Campbell Dam in the late 1980s when it was finally conceded that *squaw* was a derogatory word for an Indigenous woman. The word for woman in Swampy Cree or Nēhinawēwin is *iskwēw*, and in Ojibway or Anishinaabemowin it is *ikwe*.

The rocky bottom of the Bigstone River (Mistassini Sīpī) in the fall of 1963. The buildings pictured, from the far left, are the fish weigh station, the ice house, the Catholic Church boathouse, and the Department of Natural Resources boathouse. The smaller buildings are fishers' sheds. By the riverbank is the main dock for loading and unloading.

In the summer of 1963, meltwater from the Rocky Mountains rushing down the Saskatchewan Rivers filled the Tobin Lake reservoir, putting pressure on the newly built Squaw Rapids Dam (renamed the E.B. Campbell Dam in the late 1980s). The floodgates had to be opened, and floodwater inundated the landscape of the Cumberland Delta. The effects were dramatic downstream.

By the time this photo was taken in the fall of 1963, the hydroelectric plant had held back the water upstream, filling the reservoir behind the dam to generate electricity needed to meet increasing demand. Thus began a big draw-down for the upper Saskatchewan River Delta. Where there was once a viable commercial fishing operation for several species of fish was now left dry. Fluctuations in the water level would become common.

Photo from the Ron MacKay Collection, Northern Saskatchewan Archives, La Ronge, Saskatchewan.

During the next few and short summers after our visit to Little Cumberland, I spent more time with my dad while he conducted his land-based businesses. My older brothers had now left home for work or to pursue their secondary education, so I was my dad's helper during the months when I was not in school. During the fall, he guided hunters—mostly from Minnesota, Wisconsin, the Dakotas, and southern Saskatchewan—going after ducks and geese and moose. I didn't know it then, but this hydroelectric dam just upstream from the delta was about to change our lives in a profound way, and my dad's scarred face could not hide his concern about the changes now in sight.

WATERFOWL HUNTING
IN THE EARLY 1960S

———◇———

Goose Hunting with Conservation Officers

One weekend in October 1961 my dad organized a goose-hunting trip. It was likely the Thanksgiving weekend so I wouldn't miss school. I would have been ten years old.

My dad had invited his brother-in-law, John Morin, a patrolman for the Department of Natural Resources, Conservation Officer Ron MacKay, and a friend of Ron's. I was along on this trip as a goose caller and retriever. We all stayed at my dad's hunting camp on the Mossy River on the Friday night. The plan was to hunt all day on Saturday and return home that evening since Sundays were set aside to give the birds a reprieve from the hunters.

In the morning when we went out for the shoot, we drove up a small creek that flowed from the northwest side of Cumberland Lake into the northern shore of the Mossy River. After we had beached and tied the freighter canoes on the shore, we walked about 100 yards to the Cumberland Lake shoreline. This was an excellent goose-hunting area. It had a mudflat parallel to the Mossy River that extended to the west, all the way to Windy Lake. There were thick patches of goose grass where water had pooled from the spring through the summer without fluctuation. There were also round stands of phragmites and willows along the shoreline. The bulrushes, goose grass, and lake weeds grew well in the pools of standing water. We had good cover where we waited for the geese. We had set out the decoys before daybreak.

Then the wind picked up from the northeast (apsici kīwēcinosihk), and the geese were coming in from the west (pākisimonahk). We couldn't have asked for better hunting conditions. When the first flock came along, my dad and Uncle John did the calling. I called a few times, trying to sound like them, but I had a higher-pitched voice. When they stopped calling, I did the same. They stopped when they saw that the geese were coming for our decoys. Just as the geese came in with their webbed feet spread for landing (tōkistētēwocik), everyone got ready to shoot. Then someone called "Wait," but after a few geese landed the caller yelled "Shoot!" There were four shooters, and from that first flock of about fifty geese we gathered up ten. Each round had ten shots (six from two pump-action shotguns, four from two double-barrel shotguns), so I figured getting the ten down meant the hunters were good shooters or the shoot caller made the right call. After the first flock, another two came in, and another eight or ten geese came down each time. Since we had conservation officers among us, we stuck to the goose-hunting limit, and that hunt was over for the day after the three flocks had come in. On our way home in the afternoon, however, we went for a duck shoot.

In October 2013, when I recounted this hunting trip to my brother John, we were sitting in his Mossy River hunting lodge along with my cousin Michael McKenzie's son Robin and my son Kees Kisem. John told me that that hunting place had been a really good spot at one time, before the Cumberland Lake shoreline moved east toward Frog Island, where it is now. He said that before 1970 this hunting place was just northeast of his lodge, and he told me a bit of the area's oral history. "When Dad was a boy in the 1920s," he said, "Cumberland Lake shoreline had extended as far west as Windy Lake. [The family] lived at Pine Bluff, upstream on the Mossy River. Our grandfather would have brought him downstream to Windy Lake for their fall goose hunting." John also said that the family had also lived at Sturgeon Fisheries at one time before eventually moving to Cumberland House.

"Where Dad brought you to hunt geese was at a spot across the river from my camp. That place has changed since the 1960s," John continued. He then spoke of the history of the generations of the Carriere family who came to this part of Cumberland Lake to hunt geese. "Our dad hunted geese at Windy Lake, part of the Cumberland Lake shoreline, as a boy with his dad. You hunted geese with Dad right over there across the river from my camp. It was the old shoreline of Cumberland Lake. This year [2013] your son Kees will hunt geese with you somewhere downstream by Frog Island, where the latest Cumberland Lake shoreline is now located."

When we had travelled to John's camp, it was after the big floods of 2013. The lake's water had receded but left pools in the willowed areas behind the camp. During the night, with a full moon, the ducks were restless and moving around a lot. They were so noisy in the still of the night that we could hear them from inside the insulated cabin.

My First Canada Goose

Another trip I remember is when I had just bought my first shotgun, a single-shot 12-gauge. I believe this was in the fall of 1964, which would have made me thirteen. I was very happy with my new possession and eager to hunt geese with it. My dad decided to take me to a spot where geese were feeding, so we took a canoe one morning to the west end of Flock Bay, the southwestern extension of Cumberland Lake near his Central Angling hunting camp. It was a great location for hunting waterfowl. A creek flowed into the Central Angling and Flock Bay, and toward the south sat a huge boggy area, a ground-level sponge for rainfall and the fluctuating floodwaters that resulted from the upstream hydro dam operations. The area my dad took me to had open water with sedges, cattails, and tall clumps of phragmites. There were also lake weeds and pond lilies—it was an excellent marshland with no water control structure to suppress the water's flow.

When we got into position, my dad told me not to shoot at any ducks I saw since any geese would be frightened off and not come back to feed. We placed painted plywood goose decoys (silhouettes) out on a silt bar that had goose grass and foxtail grass growing on it, and my dad put a few inflatable rubber goose and duck decoys out on the water. We pulled the freighter canoe into the phragmites to hide it and walked around to face the decoys and wait for the geese to come. My dad said it was a good spot to set up, ēkota ōma kāpīmēhicik (it is here they have droppings), and judging from the feed the day before no doubt the geese would return to feed here that day.

The first flock came in, and my dad shot two geese down with his double-barrel shotgun. I shot but didn't get anything. Then my father told me that I should always lead the bird with the barrel and after pulling the trigger continue with a follow-through action. His famous shooting line was "Kigatasonimawāw niska tāpiskohc kāsinimawat sīsīp," meaning "Point the gun barrel at a goose like you point at a duck," which also means lead the barrel in front of the flying duck. Another flock came in, and once again my dad shot another two down. Then I finally shot one down. My first goose. I was yelling with excitement as I went to fetch it. My dad had a big smile as I brought my trophy to join the pile beside the blind. He looked very proud, and I felt even prouder.

A Whistling of Wings at Dusk

During the Thanksgiving weekend of 1965, my dad and his brother-in-law John Morin took my cousin Gerald Morin, my younger brother Clifford, and me on a waterfowl-hunting trip to the Big Eddy outfitting camp. We hunted at a place called the Steamboat Channel, where there was a mowgēwin (a gravel bar used by ducks and geese), and on the oxbow lakes on the New Channel of the Saskatchewan River. My dad had decided not to use the Big Eddy camp for his outfitting business anymore since it was being affected by water fluctuations caused by the upstream hydro dam operation. He had two other hunting lodges, one at the Central Angling River and the other at the Mossy River from which to run his outfitting business.

We beached our freighter canoes at the mouth of the Steamboat Channel and then walked to the goose gravel bars and the portage to Stump Lake. The channel had no flowing water; instead, there were small, rounded pools of shallow water. It was hard to imagine a steamboat once passing through there. Many shorebirds called sēsēsiwak (greater yellow legs) were feeding in the pools. My brother and I, with the coaxing of our uncle John, were encouraged to shoot them. We tried to sneak up on (nāscinoscigē) the birds, but every time we got close and looked over the sand ridges, they saw us right away and quickly flew off. Uncle John was amused by our sneak-up approach to hunting, as we never had a chance to shoot these elusive birds.

Eventually, however, we reached a place where a small flock of geese were gravelling. It was a calm, sunny day, and my dad and uncle knew it was too calm for shooting geese. When it is calm, it is easy for birds to hear a gunshot nearby, and waterfowl, especially geese that have been hunted before, will change where they go to feed. It was great weather for going on a stroll, but we were there to shoot birds for food. We decided to go duck hunting instead.

My uncle took his son Gerald and my younger brother Clifford, and they paddled a canoe to the southern end of Stump Lake while I stayed with my dad at the north end. We set up by a narrows to wait for ducks and pass-shoot them. Pass-shooting is when you notice or know that ducks or geese are flying over a certain location. There is no need to set up decoys. You just hide and wait for them to fly over your spot. I got impatient, though, and decided to scare some of the ducks from the shoreline, for what is called jump-shooting. I had a single-shot 12-gauge shotgun. My dad had a double barrel of the same gauge. When I walked along the shoreline, most of the ducks were out of range when I scared them up. They would then fly along the lake toward the narrows, where my dad was waiting. While jump-shooting, I did manage to shoot down some mallards, but I could never find them. I once saw my uncle Jim with his three-shot pump-action shotgun take an extra kill shot at mallards as they fell down. I realized then why he did that. Injured mallards will hide or swim away from where they fall. With my single-shot gun, I had only one kill shot, so I looked for open water where I could shoot them dead with one clean shot. I shot a blue-winged teal that had landed on an opening in the sedges, and it was an easy kill. I watched my dad at the narrows shoot down every mallard that flew within his range. My uncle and the other boys were also busy shooting.

As evening set in, it was quite calm. In the stillness of the darkening sky, there was a whistling of wings like a small tornado, and huge flocks of ducks alighted on Stump Lake. We went home with a pile of mallards (ininsipak) and gadwalls (apiscāninsipak) for both families.

THE SOUTH END OF EGG LAKE

———◇———

During the Easter break from school in 1967, when I was sixteen, we went trapping for muskrats on the southeast shore of Egg Lake in the Hudson's Bay Company Fur Lease–controlled area. I was in grade ten that year, and it was the last year I would go to school in Cumberland House since it was the last grade offered in the community. I had to leave home to finish my education, taking grade eleven in Prince Albert and grade twelve in Nipawin.

To prepare for our trip, my dad had his cousin Joe Dorion put steel strips over the wooden runners on the dogsleds. Steel, as opposed to wood, could withstand the freezing and thawing conditions of the mid-to-late spring season. I had three dogs for my sled and carried traps and wooden muskrat pelt stretchers, a shotgun, and a .22-calibre rifle. My dad had five sled dogs hitched to the jumper sled. He carried a grub box, traps, a camp stove with stove pipes, a prospector's tent, some plywood, sleeping bags, clothes, and a sixteen-foot canoe. We headed for Egg Lake, which lies almost due south of Cumberland House.

A painting of my father and me crossing Egg Lake in the spring of 1967. (The date of 1966 on the bottom of the painting should have read 1967.) Painted in the winter of 2018 at Bell's Point Elementary School in La Ronge, Saskatchewan. Tēnikī to artists John Halkett and the late Marion Ross for valuable advice and spiritual support.

Painting by Ken Carriere.

Once at the lake, we started out on the northwest shore-line, and I found myself looking at an expanse of snow that seemed to go forever into the distance. It was a sunny day, and I squinted as I looked out on the lake. Beyond its expanse, I could see a height of land, the Opasquia Hills (Pasquia Hills), which the Cumberland people called the Pas Mountain. I first saw those hills from a distance when out on Cumberland Lake, but this was the first time I saw them this close. They really did look like a mountain.

I followed my dad as he made his way to the far shore of Egg Lake. He followed no tracks. We made our own trail, but since the lake snow was hardened it was easy pulling for the dogs. They seemed to enjoy the run. They ran quickly and wagged their tails as they went along. I felt the heat of the sun on my face and enjoyed the ride across the lake.

After about two hours on the lake with no shoreline in sight, I started thinking I could see it at a distance, but I wasn't sure. My eyes seemed to play tricks on me. Suddenly, though, we arrived at the shoreline. Marsh plants emerged from the snow, and we could see many muskrat houses. This would be our trapping area. We drove into a small creek that we followed for about half a mile until we reached a campsite. This was the camp of the McKay family, and there were four people staying there: Rod McKay and his wife, Asagewin (Marie Louise), their daughter, Selina, and their son, Steve. When they weren't out on the land, the McKay family lived at Kiskāciwanohk (or Pemmican Portage), which, as I mentioned earlier, was our neighbouring settlement, on the Saskatchewan River, on the south side of Kāministikominahikoskāk (Spruce Island).

My dad quickly found a place to set up our camping gear, and within a short time we had it ready. It was evening already, with some sunlight still lingering. I gathered up some nīpisīcagosak (dried-up willows), cut them to size for firewood, and stacked them. I also went to get a bucket of water from the nearby creek. We would use it for washing and to make tea.

In a short while, Marie Louise came over and invited us to their camp for supper. She had prepared fresh bannock and a pot full of freshly smoked muskrat meat mixed with oatmeal, potatoes, carrots, and onions. There was a fresh pot of tea on the stove. We greatly enjoyed this meal and stayed to visit.

ASĀGĒWIN (FEAST)

Êgwāni pēgwāw ēsīgwāk

nigīwīcêwāw tāgīhotāwiyān

ēgīwacaskowanīgēyāk

agāmikiskāciwanohk.

This one spring

I went with my late father

we were muskrat trapping

across the Saskatchewan River.

Atimak nigīyāpaciyānānak

kīsōgipicigēwak.

We used dogs

that were strong pullers.

Tānsi mīna kāhisināgwāk

ita kāgīti itisawigēyāk?

Pēgwan māna ēsināgwak

wāsagām ēyitāpiyān.

How did it look like

where we drove the dog teams?

It looked the same

around the lake where I was looking.

Pīnisk ātawina kātipiskīkopāk.

Êkwāni kātotītamāk

ēpītikwētstikētīk sīpiy.

At last there were willow bluffs.

Then we arrived at

an opening of a river.

Kāmatēsāgāpātawēk.

Awinak ēgīmānogwēt ita.

Ispīk ēgīsi ayāpawayāstimēyāk

nigīpītigwānān pagwānigamigohk.

There was smoke.

Someone's camp is here.

*After we finished
    unharnessing the dogs*

we went inside the tent.

Êkota mêkwâc Asâgêwin tâgîtiht	*There now was Feast as she was named*
sôgi tâsîpawât wacask wayâna.	*busily stretching the muskrat skins.*
"Kimisagânâwâw.	*"You have arrived.*
Ohê! Mêsci nigisâgamisigân.	*Oh hey! I have boiled water.*
Mîcâgamin tê minîgwêk asici	*There is lots of tea, have a drink, and*
nigîgîsiswâw pâgwêsigan mêgwâc	*I have baked bannock, right now*
tâgapiw."	*it is cooling."*
Tâpwê kîminôtâgosiw.	*She sure sounded good.*
Nigînohtêgatânân. Tâpwê	*We were hungry. It sure*
kîwîgatisiw ana pâgwêsigan.	*tasted good that bannock.*

Written by Ken Carriere.

In addition to this example of the McKay's hospitality, I have several other memories of this trip. One that I clearly recall was of a fairly dangerous mishap. My father had told me to always have the mîcigiw (an ice-testing tool) in front of me while out on a frozen lake. But one day, while going about setting traps in the muskrat houses, I started carrying the tool on my shoulder and not in front of me as I was told. I found out then that the advice my father had given me was solid and that the ice was not, at least not enough to carry my weight. I went through the ice and did not feel the bottom. I was submerged up to my neck. Thanks to the mîcigiw, however, I pulled myself out of the water back onto the ice surface. I was all alone—the only witnesses I had were the sled dogs. When they heard my struggling noises, they looked up

My depiction of falling through lake ice after failing to properly carry my mīcigiw (ice-testing tool).

Painting by Ken Carriere.

from their sleep but went right back to taking a nap. I wrung out my clothes, put them back on, and continued setting the few traps I had left. I then got the sled dogs to take me back to camp, and they did the famous, enthusiastic "we are going home now" routine. The sun was just overhead, and the air temperature was just above freezing. Within a few minutes of getting to camp, I was back in our tent and firing up the belly stove. I changed into dry clothes and hung the wet ones up to dry beside the stove.

ON THE SACRED GRASSBERRY

◇

I n spring 1973, I made arrangements with my father to spend the summer at home. I had been taking undergraduate courses in geological sciences at an English university in Montreal and had experienced two summers doing on-the-ground surveys with the Saskatchewan Department of Mineral Resources as a geologist's assistant. But this summer I would work for my father, helping him with his commercial fishing business, cabin building, and other projects. For the commercial fishing enterprise, we went to a pair of adjoining lakes, located southwest of Amisk Lake in east-central Saskatchewan. The eastern lake is known as Windy Lake; the western one we call Cācagi or Sasagi Sākahigan, but it appears on maps as Suggi Lake. This trip was special in many ways. I travelled with my great-uncle Albert (Ānipats) Flett and my brother John in a freighter canoe with a ten-horse-power Johnson outboard motor, and to get to the lakes we had to travel up the Grassberry River, which had many rapids. The river was navigable, though, during the spring melt or if there was high water during the summer or fall.

The Grassberry is one of the main routes followed by travellers from the Saskatchewan River system heading north. Going northeast, via Windy Lake, you can connect to Amisk Lake and the Sturgeon-weir River, from where you can continue toward Wāpāwikosciganihk (also known as Pelican Narrows) and then the Churchill River. My brother John said that, by going northwest via Suggi Lake, you could reach Achinnini (Blackfoot) Lake, connect to Limestone Lake, and then Kimosōmpwātināhk (Deschambault Lake), the Cree name meaning among the grandfather Sioux or place of the ancient Sioux. From there, you can continue west to Wapawekka Lake, which lies off the southeastern flank of Lac La Ronge. The name Wapawekka is a version of Northern Plains Cree; in my own Swampy Cree language, we call it Wāpinēgwa, which translated into English means white sand.

On our trip from Cumberland House to the Grassberry, we went up the New Channel of the Central Angling River and then turned west through the Sturgeon Fisheries. This once famous landscape, however, was now a set of channels and no longer resembled a lake. We then came to a place called Kāgēskiciwak (where the river current runs opposite to the main channel), where the Mossy River enters the Sturgeon Fisheries. From there, we went upstream on the Mossy toward Ministikwācagsihk, also known as Pine Bluff, where my father was from, just below the confluence of the Grassberry River. On the way, I managed to shoot down two fall ducks (maskēgosipak or lesser scaup) while I sat at the front of the canoe, so we stopped at Pine Bluff for a lunch break, cooking the ducks in Albert's cooking pot. Albert put in carrots, potatoes, onions, and parts of the ducks, and after letting it boil for several minutes he put in two handfuls of oatmeal to thicken the mix, making duck soup. After this meal, we had a fresh pot of tea with sugar and milk, along with bannock with lard and Rogers Golden Syrup.

After we ate lunch, several more canoes with other fishermen came up the Grassberry with us. John ran the

Fishermen poling upstream on the Grassberry River rapids in twenty-foot freighter canoes. The canoes had wooden ribs and painted canvas covers, and could be powered by ten-horsepower outboard motors. This photograph was taken at a place called the Ten Mile Rapids.

Photo from the Ron Mackay Collection, Northern Saskatchewan Archives, La Ronge, Saskatchewan.

outboard motor up the river. It became narrow, the rapids came into view, and then our adventures began. John had been there before, so we followed his instructions. We began the agwāgosiwin (poling) using long poles to push ourselves up the rapids. We travelled as a group and met my uncle James Carriere and his partner, Jean Baptiste Laliberte, along the way. My friend Steve McAuley was travelling in another canoe with his brother Joseph. Altogether there were about ten canoes. I remember my great-uncle Albert's comment about how well I conducted myself in this adventure, being the bowman. Only once did we get into trouble with the current when the bow swung out too far sideways into the fast current and nearly upset the canoe. Afterward, I took care not to get sideswiped again by the rushing current.

Looking back, I recall a saying in Cree that describes a person who is clumsy in a canoe, someone prone to tipping it over. My father told me it related to Euro-Canadians and originated during their initial contact with North American Indigenous Peoples. The Cree word is mōniyāw, derived from the phrase ēmōniyāwnigēt, which describes someone who is clumsy and does things without care and attention. Mōniyāw, however, was originally an inclusive term and described not only Euro-Canadians (white people), though many Cree might now use the term mōnyāw (reworded to mōniyās) when referring to white people specifically. I recall that I was called a mōnyāw only once during our trip.

The time spent with my great-uncle Albert reminded me of when we went canoeing around Pine Island looking for moose during the summer flood of 1963. I was twelve years old on that trip and had just started to learn how to paddle a canoe; on this trip, I was twenty-two and had much more experience with canoeing, running outboard motors, and dealing with lake and river travel in general. But this journey going up a set of rapids in a narrow river floodplain was my first such trip, and I had to learn fast. I carefully listened to instructions as they were shouted to me above the noise of the rapids.

Along the way, we saw a moose shedding its winter coat, looking bloody from the ticks that had burrowed into its hide. We all felt sorry for that moose. My brother John told me that moose usually shed their winter coats in early May and might then have patches of their hides exposed, leaving them vulnerable to being attacked by every blood-sucking insect there is. I could only think then of the moose as the provider for all life forms in these northern woods, from insects to people. At home at Cumberland House, we often got our moose meat from ōta oci nōcimihk, meaning from these hunting grounds here.

Farther along the journey upstream on the Grassberry River, we came upon a rise of land. With my training in geo-logical sciences, I was familiar with the rock types of the

Canadian Shield we encountered. We were on a plateau and an outcrop of smooth crystalline rock. It was a coarse-grained grey granite of the Precambrian Age on top of which lay Paleozoic Age limestone. I could only imagine what the large continental ice sheet of the last ice age did to scrape out this landscape.

Our group stopped for the day at a place sheltered by tall white spruce, an old campsite where travellers had stayed in the past. It was known as kāpēgowastēhk, meaning a place where a single rapids was bordered by calm waters upstream and downstream. Everyone pitched a tent (mānogēwak) and made a campfire (kotawēwak). This was the only time all of us river travellers would get to camp together. All you heard after everyone had eaten supper was the sound of laughter. The older men told stories, and there was a lot of friendly teasing. It was May 8, 1973, and we got caught up in a transistor radio broadcast of a Stanley Cup playoff game. The teams playing were the Montreal Canadiens and the Chicago Blackhawks. We sipped fresh tea, visited, and listened to the play-by-play. I recall that I once wore the Blackhawks jersey depicting an Indigenous warrior's head on it without thinking of the negativity behind it, but when I was educated about the colonization of the Indigenous Peoples in the Americas, I came to realize the disrespect that the jersey carried.

The written record states that our Indigenous ("red") race was defeated by a Euro–North American ("white") race whose civilization they considered way more superior than ours. They had no qualms about using our colonized, displaced, and disrespected red race for their sports teams' names or portraying us unflatteringly in their logos. Such white race acts are correctly described as racist and culturally arrogant. I have heard arguments about the inappropriateness of using names of Indigenous Peoples for sports teams. Many teams use logos depicting the Indigenous Peoples of North America. In one interview, I heard a comment on the wearing of the Chicago Blackhawks jersey. It came from a member of an electronic music band named A Tribe Called Red. In their live concerts, fans would show up wearing Blackhawks jerseys. The band member said he was not sure that their fans should be wearing those jerseys. I gather he didn't want to see such a display.

The name Black Hawk was that of a leader of the Sauk People who lived in western Illinois. The Sauk were allied with the Ojibway of Michigan and the Odawa Nation around Georgian Bay. The Odawa called them Osaugeek (or Sauk). Black Hawk defended his people from ethnic cleansing by American western expansionists. Historically, Indigenous people were either shot on sight or rounded up and then herded at gunpoint onto reservations. In his Osaugeek language, Warrior Chief Black Sparrow Hawk carried the name Mà-ka-tai-me-she-kià-kiàk. How about using his Osaugeek name for your sports team?

The morning after visiting and listening to the Stanley Cup playoffs, we were up at the crack of dawn. Soon campfires were crackling and coffee was brewing; we fried our bacon and eggs, had breakfast, and were ready to continue on our way. From this point on the Grassberry, we were able to run the outboard motor, and in no time we reached the entrance to Sākahigan (or Windy Lake), the eastern twin to Suggi Lake. At the confluence was a large limestone boulder, and every traveller in each canoe placed an offering on this rock (asiniy). I asked my brother John what that was about. He said it was spiritual, a ritual passed on by a respected medicine man named Sēpincēk who lived at Ministigwācagāsihk (or Pine Bluff) for most of his life. This ritual was about giving thanks to the Creator for having reached this spot, and it was hoped that this humble gesture would keep you safe as you went farther on, and that your spiritual helper might provide a good harvest from the lakes. I was now introduced to the spiritual practices of my ancestors, and I gave my thanks like everyone else.

This ritual made me feel more connected to the land, and it was the beginning of a transcendence for me. I believe there is no need to rationalize such rituals or any ritual for that matter—leave it to the believers, and let them have their moments of reflection. This passing by the boulder made me begin to realize that there exists another level of awareness. This ritual was a reminder to be humble and to reach toward a higher power for guidance. Perhaps because of my companions' offerings at the boulder, I felt a strong connection to Windy Lake and Chachuggi Sakahigan (Suggi Lake) as soon as we left the Grassberry. This was my dad's trapping area. It was where Dad made his living and where he brought home much that we needed. At Suggi Lake, we stayed at his trapping cabin, but we ate our meals at my uncle Jim's place, a cozy cabin for both trapping and winter fishing. Trapping cabins are called wāskahiganisa in our Cree. The other fishermen camped in canvas tents (pakwānigamigwa) on a large wooded island (ministik) called Dougal's Island, my grandfather Dougal McKenzie's place. Nearby was another island, a rocky one (ministikwāpisk) where colonies of pelicans and gulls were nesting.

My dad was the main organizer of this cooperative fishing venture to Suggi and Windy Lakes. He had the business sense and kept an accounting ledger, but he was also involved as a fisherman, maintaining a fishing licence for the lakes. He was behind the concept of local control of commercial fishing on certain lakes and involved other fishermen, making sure that the Cumberland House men also had their licences to operate on Suggi and Windy Lakes. But while most of us had made the run up the Grassberry, my dad and my brother Franklin had the privilege of being flown in from Cumberland House.

After Dad arrived, he wasted no time getting us out onto the water, and we set nets at places where he thought the whitefish would be swimming in schools. The lake water was shallow enough, only about five feet deep, so we used anchor poles (cīstapānātikwa) twenty feet in length. Each pole would stick up five feet above the water, sit in water five feet deep, and be anchored into the lake bottom mud to about ten feet. We had six gillnets out, each 100 yards long with a five-inch mesh. Setting one net took at least fifteen to twenty minutes depending on the wind. Getting the anchor poles to take hold was the most time-consuming part of setting the net. Despite being muddy, the bottom was still quite hard, so the anchor pole had a sharpened point. We would then rock the freighter canoe, and the motion, along with the weight of the pole setter, would eventually get the pole into place. Three nets would be set between four anchor poles. If there was no wind to create choppy waves, then everything went well; otherwise, it was quite a task to keep the nets set straight. Setting nets with their anchor poles in line like a surveyor (tipāskāta, meaning line it up) was something fishermen took pride in.

The prized commercial fish we were after were jumbo whitefish; when we checked the nets later and found fewer than ten in each, it was time to pull those nets out and move to another location. One problem was too many lake suckers. They were starting to come back into the lakes after their spawning runs in the creek beds and getting into our nets.

To get our fish out to the fish plant at Amisk Lake, a pilot, Joan Struder, from La Ronge, was hired. She stayed at one of my uncle Jim's cabins and would get started early each morning, making about four round trips each day since it was a short flight to Amisk Lake and back. She would get someone to help her unload the fish there and then stay around to get the weigh master to record the catch total. Then she would bring back the record slips and any supplies requested. This operation lasted over two weeks, about the time needed to reach the catch limit set for the Suggi Lake–Windy Lake spring fishing season. Once the operation was shut down, we went home.

The run downstream on the Grassberry River took only about three hours, but it was even shorter if we ran the outboard motor, which we could do in most places while the river was running high from the spring runoff. In at least one place, though, we had to shut off the motor and use paddles to help us steer around large boulders and to stay on the deeper channel. Comparing how long it took to come upstream on the Grassberry, the run downstream seemed like time travel. Who could not enjoy such a trip?

THE REVERED MOOSE

———————◇———————

Besides the introduction to traditional spirituality I felt upon my arrival at Suggi and Windy Lakes, I had reason for another strong connection. As I mentioned, this was my father's trapping area. After two months there each winter, Dad usually came home on an old winter trail that he had cleared himself. It cut across a big muskeg south of Suggi Lake and joined the upper Mossy River by the Pine Bluff Indian Reserve, where he grew up. He would make this trip just before Christmas. He would then follow the Mossy River to Snake Point on the northwest end of Cumberland Lake, and as he made his way along the river he usually hunted moose if he saw fresh tracks in the snow. If successful, he would kill the moose, dress the kill, and take the choice parts—such as the upper part of the digestive tract below the stomach (mitagisiy), the heart (mitēh), kidneys (tōtōkosiya), liver (oskōn), tongue (mitēnaniy), and hindquarters (osōganiya)—and add them to the load on his toboggan sled. A few days after getting home, he would go back to nigaciso, meaning get the meat from a kill, which he usually stored at my great-uncle Albert Flett's trapping cabin at Snake Point.

To us, the moose was one of the most important animals, and my brother Franklin once told me a story of an impressive moose hunt he witnessed while trapping with Dad. While they were setting beaver traps on Windy Lake, our father spotted a moose eating along a bay on the northern shore. He decided to hunt the animal. Franklin watched as Dad crawled along on his hands and knees quietly and quickly toward the moose. Normally, when a trapper goes hunting moose, he uses a rifle larger than .22 calibre, but Dad had just a .22-calibre repeating rifle with a fifteen-bullet magazine, but at least it had a bolt action that ejected the casing while another bullet was pushed into the barrel ready to be fired. With his stealth, Dad got very close to the moose before it knew he was there. He started shooting the moose in its front side and kept shooting at the same spot until the moose started bleeding from its mouth. Dad was then able to get close to give it the final kill shots. In my interview with my brother Franklin later in this book, he recounts the story, telling me how he watched how this moose was killed, dressed, and then stored securely overnight in a bush area full of wolves and other hungry animals.

I asked my brother John where our father had learned these hunting skills. John said that often while in the bush country trappers encountered wolves or signs of their activity, and if a trapper was shrewd enough he could learn from them. And wolves were always hunting moose. A wolf's main tactic was to sneak up to the moose from downwind before its presence was felt, since a moose, even while feeding or resting, is always on the lookout for wolves. The wolf had to outwit the internal sentinel of the moose, and what worked for a wolf could work for a trapper. This was the case with my father with the .22-calibre rifle he carried while on the trapline, as all trappers do. There is not much need for stealth with a high-calibre rifle; at a relatively close distance, a moose can be taken down quickly with a clear-range shot.

I mention the taking of moose with great respect. My mother held this forest animal in reverence, as did all Indigenous women who fed their children moose meat. I learned its value from my mother at an early age. We were toddlers and youngsters when my father would head home for Christmas from his trapline at Suggi and Windy Lakes, and my mother would tell us to look out the north window of our house to see if we could spot his dog team driving onto the shores of Cumberland Lake. Somehow, though, Mom would always see the dog team on the lakeshore before we did, and she would then tell us to put hay bedding inside the doghouses. I think that perhaps my parents had what I like to think of as Cree telepathy (there were no two-way radios or cellphones in their time), because Mom knew a day or two before Dad and his dog team would arrive. Most Cree would say, however, ēgīgiskimāt ana owīgimāgana (he had promised his spouse that date). It was fun for us kids to look out for Dad after he was gone all that time, and when he got home we would have a supper of fresh moose heart roasted in the oven. Dad would even treat his dogs with a bit of moose meat from the hindquarters.

When I was old enough to visit other people in our settlement, I experienced a further value of the moose. During the summer months, my dad's relatives and friends from the Pine Bluff Indian Reserve would come and spend the summer in Cumberland House. Everyone would arrive in canoes, and usually they would mānoge (set up camp) along the Bigstone River or on the Cumberland Lake shoreline beside the fire tower. Chief Tom Settee and his wife, my dad's aunt Adele, would stay in a cabin by the Bigstone River; the others stayed in tents.

For food, everyone would hunt moose, ducks, and geese, and they would fish throughout the summer—as registered (or Status) Treaty Indians, they were allowed to practise subsistence hunting. As non-registered (or Non-Status) Treaty Indians, we were not allowed to hunt moose out of season during the summer months; however, we could trade with the Treaty Indians for their moose meat. The Pine Bluff people were well known to my mom, and she would send me to trade things like a pound of lard, a bag of sugar, or tea or coffee for moose meat. Someone would have told my mother that someone else had arrived who had moose meat they were willing to trade, and I would show up and always get a real welcome from these people on account of her.

These people knew my mom by her nickname, Sōminis, given to her by her grandfather (omosōma) Louis Jourdain. When my mother was a baby, her navel became infected, and Louis went around looking for a raisin to place in her navel, believing it would heal her infection. His search for raisins in the community led to the nickname, which stuck with her for much of her life. My bartering on behalf of Sōminis complete, the moose meat I took home felt precious.

I would often return to the campsites of the Pine Bluff visitors since I found instant friends there, boys my own age to play with. Among the group was the family of Alex Morin, one of my dad's relatives. Alex's wife had passed away, and he raised his family as a widower. He always had a smile and was very kind, and I enjoyed learning bush skills from him and his sons. I spent many summers with one of his sons, David, whose nickname I fondly recall was Pigiloose.

PIGILŌS

Ēgwāni pēyagwāw ēnīpihk	This one summer
Nigīwīcimētawēmāw mīcētwāw	I played with him many times
awa kāyācmak.	this person whom I am telling about.
Pigilōs ēgītiht, Miniscikwācagasihk oci.	His name was Pigiloose, he was from Pine Bluff.

Pogītē māna nōcimihk nigītōtānān,	We went all over the bushes,
Kawpanīy sagāk, āpaskwāskihk,	Company woods, the meadows,
cīgi sāgahiganihk,	along the lakeshore,
ēgwa Minsicigwācasihk ininiwi kapēsiwin.	and the Pine Bluff people's campsite.

Êgī papāmi nōcipinēsīsiwēyāk.	We went about hunting birds.
Pasicigēpicigan ēgīyāpacītāyāk.	A slingshot we would use.

Êhē nigiskisin nicēwāganis Pigilōs.	I remember my little friend Pigiloose.
Mistawi nigīmōcigītānān nōcimihk.	We had a lot of fun in the bushes.
Êgī papāmi nōciyāgwak pinēsīsak.	We would go around killing birds.

Êgwāni māna ogotawānihk	Then at his campfire place
kāgīcīpātawayāgwak anigi	we would roast those
kāgīnīpēgawisowak.	that we killed for food.
Nīstanān ēgīwīgispāwayāgwak.	We enjoyed eating them too.

First written by Ken Carriere in 1992, revised July 24, 2014.

LAMBAIR TO GET WELL,
GO HOME ON "BOMBADEER"

◇

I
n February 1961, when I was just shy of my tenth birthday, I had appendicitis. It was during a snowstorm that
lasted for two days, so I was lucky to get taken by airplane to The Pas, Manitoba, where there was a hospital. I
had been running a high fever and experiencing convulsions,
and I couldn't even walk since I felt almost paralyzed. My
brother John had to put me on a dogsled and take me out
onto Cumberland Lake, for a break in the storm had allowed
the plane affixed with skis to land. I flew with the legendary
Tom Lamb's Lambair service stationed in The Pas and had
emergency surgery later that day. I remember being put to
sleep with laughing gas and later waking up to a young, red-
haired woman who was my nurse. I had a severe pain in the
right side of my abdomen and had black surgical stitches
where I had been opened up to remove the ruptured appendix. I began to get better within a few days and started getting visitors: my dad, my uncle William and aunt Josephine,
among other relatives. I also remember that my nurse came
in with a copy of *The Pas Herald* newspaper with the great
news that my uncle Bill Carriere had just won the World

The Bombardier snow tracker sitting in the background is the same type I was transported in to Cumberland House a week after surgery to remove my appendix. Uncle John Morin is at left holding an ice chisel while setting a net for winter fishing on Cumberland Lake. Uncle John later became a conservation officer serving at Weyakwin, Saskatchewan.

Photo from the Ron Mackay Collection, Northern Saskatchewan Archives, La Ronge, Saskatchewan.

Championship Dog Race in The Pas, discussed later in this book in my interviews with my cousin Margaret Schweitzer and my brother John Victor.

But my adventures with my recovery were just about to begin. When I was released from the hospital, I joined a group of people travelling back to Cumberland House through the Birch River settlement, about halfway between The Pas and our community. We took a covered snow tracker made by Bombardier, which the locals called "Bombadeer." It was a very bumpy ride, and the first snowdrift we hit jolted the tracker, causing a sharp pain where I'd had my surgery. After that, I grabbed the edge of the bench I was sitting on and lifted myself up to avoid those jolts as we continued over the rough terrain.

Some years later my aunt Marie Louise McKenzie told me that she'd had a similar medivac experience when she'd had appendicitis. She told me the story when I visited her at St. Paul's Hospital in Saskatoon when she was getting ready for another surgery. She said that upon a physical examination the surgeon was astounded at the number of her surgical scars. It was then that I asked her if she ever had appendicitis. She said that she was also flown to St. Anthony's Hospital in The Pas, the same hospital that I was at, and recalled instantly the Bombadeer ride back home post-surgery. We shared a similar experience.

MY FATHER'S KNOWLEDGE
OF THE SOUTHERN PLAINS

◇

n the spring of 1978, I drove my father to a place called Oskana Kāsastēki (Pile of Bones) or what is known today as Regina, "the Queen City." My co-driver was my cousin Philip Fosseneuve, nicknamed "Red," my uncle Isidore Carriere's grandson. My father was going to Regina for surgery to get a pin to hold up his jaw. This trip took us through the Qu'Appelle Valley just west of the Piapot Indian Reserve. In our Cree, this place is called Pēyapwāt, which I was told meant where we wait for the Pwātak-Dakotas or Sioux Tribe Peoples.

My dad told us that during the winter the Paskwā mostosak (Great Plains bison herds) would go down into the valley to escape the severe winter storms. I wondered how my father, a northern bush Cree person, would know these things. My brother John told me that our nōkominān (grandmother) Agnes Morin had been a student at the Lebret Indian Residential School in the valley near Fort Qu'Appelle; additionally, my mom, Agnes, had spent some time at the tuberculosis hospital in the Fort Qu'Appelle area, Fort San. Indigenous people were sent to sanatoriums when government medical authorities suspected that they had tuberculosis. My mom did not have TB, but she still ended up at Fort San. Fortunately, she left before she contracted the sickness. So perhaps my mother and grandmother had learned something about what life was like on the plains and passed it on to my father.

I also once met a Métis gentleman with the surname Parisien from Fort Qu'Appelle who told me that he knew my father. He said that my father had travelled from Cumberland House to Nipawin, where he then took a bus to Regina to attend Métis Society of Saskatchewan meetings (today the organization is known as Métis Nation—Saskatchewan). He also said that my father had arranged a meeting with the then-premier of Saskatchewan, Ross Thatcher, to talk about getting Métis farms started at Cumberland House like those that had been established at Lebret.

The Non-Status Indians and Métis of southern Saskatchewan near Lebret were the last group of Great Plains bison hunters—they supplied bison meat to be processed into pemmican during the fur trade era—so it was also possible that my dad learned about the habits of the Paskwā mostosak during that trip.

I also learned that my dad knew about the histories of the Cree, Dakota, Ojibway, and Métis during the fur trade era and that the business of supplying bison meat was forever displaced by the building of the transcontinental railway and the coming of eastern Canadian and British Isles settlers, who came to colonize western Canada by homesteading on land claimed by the British crown—despite the fact that there were already people living there.

1979

———————◇———————

I remember the early part of 1979 for two reasons. The first is that on February 26, 1979, a solar eclipse was visible throughout western Canada. Southeastern Saskatchewan and central Manitoba experienced a total eclipse, but Cumberland House was well within range to view a partial eclipse. I bought two pairs of welder's goggles and went to visit my parents. My dad and I stood in his driveway to watch this celestial event. It was almost a year after our trip to Regina for his corrective surgery to fix his drooping jaw.

My second memory isn't as pleasant. Later that spring my father started getting chest pains and was hospitalized in Nipawin for a heart condition. I went with my brother Clifford and cousin Ordean Goulet to visit him, and in July he passed away at the age of sixty-three. In the years that passed, my mother often mentioned the surgery that he'd had for his jaw, and I remember her saying, "Anawāc otē kīpamīcigātēnik mīna owīgwāgan" ("They should have fixed his heart instead of his face"). When I mentioned these words to my aunt Elise Sayese, she replied, "Your mom was right. Your dad could have lived a bit longer if they had fixed his heart. I had a heart

Pierre Carriere at the hospital in Nipawin, 1979.

Photo courtesy of Ordean Goulet, Saskatoon, Saskatchewan.

attack, and after open heart surgery they made my heart work better. My sister Marie Louise, she had open heart surgery, and she got better too." What a revelation that was to me. Two of my aunts, who had given birth to many children, were able to continue with their lives as great-grandmothers (châpâns in Cree). Both have now reached over ninety years of standing on Mother Earth.

The thought of how resilient my aunties are makes me recall a certain lesson I was taught. I was listening to a Cree elder who had come to the school where I was working with youth and young adults, and he advised the young men present to respect all women as they respected their own mothers. He told them that by nature women are stronger than men. This Cree elder was a tall, strong-looking man, and when he told the group this they gave him a quizzical look. He then gave them the reason for his statement. Women had to be stronger than men in order to give birth to babies and raise them, he said, adding that men didn't have the same burdens; however, they could be given strong hearts by their mothers. Then, with their strong hearts and knowledge and training, men could defend their people when under attack. The understanding of these strengths has been with people worldwide from the time when they lived in clan societies, the elder said. In my parents' time, our people were two generations removed from clan societies, but still, when tyranny threatened the world and people were called to war, my dad and his brothers followed that clan society reasoning and enlisted for the war effort. Their hearts were strong then.

HOMAGE TO LENA STEWART

———◇———

One calm summer evening in early August 1997, I gave my mother a ride to see Cumberland Lake from the Tearing River landing. I knew she would like the view. It was then that she said in Cree "Tāpwē pīkiskācināgwan" ("It sure looks calm and peaceful"). On our way back to the village of Cumberland House, where she lived, we dropped in on a good friend of my mother, Lena Stewart (née Greenleaf), who lived on the Cumberland House First Nation. There's a saying in Indian country: "Drop by, don't be a stranger." If you don't feel guilty after hearing that plea, then maybe you haven't lived yet. I try my best to follow this advice. Lena was the niece of Sēpincēk (see the chapters "On the Sacred Grassberry" and "Where Prayers Are Called Upon"), and like her uncle she was a knowledge keeper who practised traditional medicine. I wrote a commemoration of this visit.

I heard about her she was a maskīgī iskwēw (medicine woman).
She wanted to know who I was before I could introduce myself.
I am here with my mother, Sōminis, I said, and then she smiled.

I could tell by their conversation they were old friends.

They had never said anything wrong of each other.

We began our conversation while she cut moose ribs.

She took great care to clean the bone fragments from the meat.

She said, "The sharp fragments are dangerous for small children.

These are easy to swallow and can make someone very sick."

Her hands held the meat like it was the most precious thing.

Her wrinkled face smiled as she continued to cut and clean.

I felt fortunate that I understood and spoke her language.

I was thankful for my mother, who had such wise and beautiful friends.

In Lena's voice, I heard no moral indignation.

She said, "It is not important in what you do wrong,

somehow sometimes you do what is right."

She had an answer for everything I asked her.

On opigīyāwasowin (raising children) with kindness and love,

a mother will have her children coming back to see her.

They passed on some old medicine stories to each other.

"Keeping a skunk in your house is healthy.

The air is cleansed of germs

whenever the scent rises from the skunk's sack.

Only one thing to remember.

A skunk is not a pet for everyone, just that one person.

It can always sense if you are a nasty type.

Don't try to pet one if you are mean."

My mother told me, when I was an infant, she gave me a drink.

It was a mix of hot water and oil from a skunk's scent bag.

I never once suffered vicious colds as an infant.

UNCLE ROGER'S LEGACY

◇

n my youth, I enjoyed canoe racing, and as I mentioned earlier, when my brother Clifford became a father, he taught his children the sport. I was inspired by the local paddlers of Cumberland House, Pine Bluff, Sturgeon Landing, Opaskwayak Cree Nation, Cranberry Portage, and Flin Flon. My uncle Roger Carriere, who has since entered the spirit world, was the catalyst for all those great canoe racers in their day. He challenged them and taught them how to train. He also competed in the Northern Manitoba King Trapper events in The Pas, winning the title of King Trapper fourteen times between 1954 and 1975. He won many additional titles at festivals in places such as Edmonton, Alberta, and Thompson, Manitoba. My brother Franklin and his friends at Sled Lake, Green Lake, La Ronge, Stanley Mission, Grandmother's Bay, Moose Lake, Cormorant, Cumberland House, and Opaskwayak Cree Nation all enjoyed competing with each other in the King and Queen Trapper competitions in the winter festivals of northern Saskatchewan and Manitoba. Franklin developed his competitive spirit with encouragement from Uncle Roger.

Later I became involved in the training of inner-city youth for canoe racing with the Regina Canoe Club coordinated by Rick Cardinal. Many of those I trained had qualified for the North American Indigenous Games (NAIG) to be held in 1999 in Fargo, North Dakota, my son Nathan Arthur Carriere Niskala included. The Fargo games, however, were sadly cancelled because of the long-term effects of the flooding of the Red River in the state. Twenty years later, in 2019, tryouts for canoe and kayak racing were held in Prince Albert, Saskatoon, and Regina for the 2020 NAIG to be held in Halifax. I recall attending some of these tryouts and encouraging some of the competitors to paddle harder, saying that if they did they would please the spirit of Uncle Roger. My son Kees Kisem Carriere and his cousin Blaze Carriere were picked as alternates for the team of youths that qualified for the C-2 canoe race (C-2 meaning a canoe with two paddlers), but unfortunately the NAIG scheduled for the summer of 2020 were cancelled due to the COVID-19 pandemic. Talk about unlucky timing for my sons Nathan and Kees.

My knowledge of Uncle Roger Carriere came from those who knew him. My cousin, his daughter, Beverly Carriere, whom I visited in Cranberry Portage, Manitoba, in March 2020, was kind enough to share memories of her father as well as many photographs that he took. He was an avid photographer, particularly of hunting guides and hunters. My cousin also demonstrated one of the training techniques that my uncle used to keep in shape. One end of a bungee cord is attached to a solid basement pole and the other to a paddle handle. The paddle stroke is emulated and practised to keep the right muscles in tone.

My cousin Glen Dubinak was a canoe racer with the Flin Flon paddlers training out at Phantom Lake, just south of the city. When I told him that my son Kees was training there with the Flin Flon Nordic Ski and Marathon Canoe Club, Glen said he used to bike from his home at Creighton to go paddle

Roger Carriere, wearing the moosehide beaded jacket created by his sister Marie Alma Morin, getting ready for the twenty-five-mile snowshoe race at The Pas Trapper's Festival, circa 1960. His taller competitor is wearing moosehide beaded mukluks with fur trim and tassels made by a Cree woman from his home community. Roger's nephew Jimmy Goulet is in the background facing the camera.

Courtesy of Beverly Carriere, Cranberry Portage, Manitoba.

Three generations of canoe race competitors. From left to right: Lionel McKenzie (2nd generation), Real Carriere (3rd generation), Roger Carriere (1st generation), and Solomon Carriere (2nd generation).

Photo by Rene Carriere, courtesy of Beverly Carriere, Cranberry Portage, Manitoba.

there. Glen and my brother Franklin also competed against Uncle Roger in the Centennial Voyageur Canoe Pageant in 1967. It was a race of more than 4,800 kilometres from Rocky Mountain House, Alberta, to Montreal, Quebec. Glen and Franklin were chosen to paddle with the Saskatchewan team. Another Cumberland House paddler, Napoleon Laliberte, was on the Northwest Territories team. Uncle Roger paddled with the Manitoba team in the fourth seat of the canoe—one of the two "power seats" along with Joe Michel of Sturgeon Landing—and the Manitoba team won the race by days. Glen had great praise for Roger and said, "He was always a kind person and a true gentleman."

Uncle Roger was our hero. He danced the Red River jig with his beaded moosehide jacket on while the fringes swayed and the fox tail fur hood lining wagged to meet the beat. His fancy steps on tasselled beaded mukluks followed the fiddle tune with the smoothness of a spectacle. He paddled in the world's longest marathon canoe race to celebrate the Confederation of Canada in the centennial year of 1967. He and his fellow Cree paddler Joe Michel anchored and advised the Manitoba canoe team during that epic journey. They showed their fellow paddlers the power stroke that gave them an edge over their rivals. Uncle Roger's hunting and fishing skills guaranteed a steady supply of fresh meat. His trapping skills led to prime pelts for the fur market and gave Uncle Roger cash above the wages he earned as a railway worker.

In the words of my sister Anne, Uncle Roger was a "cultural icon." He was also a great ambassador. He travelled to many Canadian and American cities demonstrating his knowledge of the north, representing the Indigenous Peoples of North America to American and Canadian television audiences. He appeared on the CBS television show *To Tell the Truth* and on many episodes of *Sesame Street*. This was at a time when the Canadian-born Cree singer Buffy Sainte-Marie was highlighting Indigenous content on children's television. Roger's TV role was that of an elder who demonstrated his cultural activities and carefully studied wild animal behaviour while on field excursions with curious children. Uncle Roger played his role as a natural. I say "Good pick, Buffy!" if she did recommend him.

WHERE PRAYERS ARE CALLED UPON

◇

I t is said that when Christian missionaries first came to the Ininiwak (the People), many accepted their faith. They became known as the Christian Ininiwak or the Christian People. They were identified as *les Cristianaux* by the French fur traders, a name later shortened to *les Cris*, which the English in turn translated to Cree, still our present name in their language.

Western churches had been trying to convert the Cree in Cumberland House to Christianity as far back as 1840, when an Anglican mission was established by catechist Henry Budd, a Swampy Cree, who later became the first ordained Anglican minister of First Nations ancestry in North America. Following the Red River insurrection in 1869–70, a number of Manitoba Métis came to the Cumberland district, and a Roman Catholic mission was established to serve these newcomers. Decades later we were raised attending the Catholic Church. My mother attended it regularly and made sure we did too. I have often considered how her spirituality was passed on to me and my siblings.

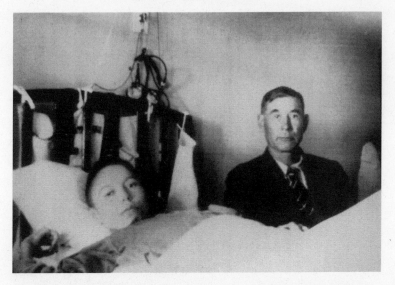

Mosōm Dougal McKenzie sitting beside his son Donald's hospital bed in Prince Albert.

Photo courtesy of Les Carriere, Cumberland House.

I received my confirmation in the Catholic Church, became an altar boy, and received the sacrament. I attended and served Sunday Mass both morning and evening, the First Friday of the Month Mass, and all other church functions. We had a priest in a rectory, nuns in a convent. On some Sunday mornings, but not that often, my father attended church. I think he did so to satisfy my mother, but maybe it was to show respect for our popular priest, Father Trudeau. He went beyond his religious duties and was involved in gardening, hunting, and coaching men's hockey, and he encouraged the nuns to open the rectory to regular catechism classes. Brothers and nuns from the order taught, respectively, the boys woodworking and the girls baking, sewing, and cooking.

My mother was very devout, attending all the days of worship celebrated at the church, and she had personal

Dougal McKenzie's first wife, my biological maternal grandmother, Virginie Jourdain, is second from the left. Far left is her sister, Catherine Umpherville (née Jourdain), and on the right are my great-grandparents, Louis Jourdain and Marguerite Jourdain (née McKay). Photo taken at Cumberland House, Northwest Territories, in 1900.

Photo courtesy of Saskatchewan Archives, image S-B9788.

reasons for making a daily pilgrimage. There was a cemetery between the convent and the church where her biological parents were buried and where, as a child, I first saw human remains. It was when we were digging a grave for my mother's father, my grandfather Dougal McKenzie, who was to be buried beside his first wife, Virginie Jourdain. We inadvertently unearthed the skeletal remains of my mother's younger brother, Donald McKenzie, who had contracted tuberculosis and been institutionalized at the Prince Albert Sanatorium, where he died at the age of fourteen. We all became even more spiritual after uncovering his remains,

Photo of nimosōminān (our grandfather) Dougal McKenzie taken at the Sturgeon-weir River.

Photo courtesy of Mike and Kate Dubinak, Creighton, Saskatchewan.

My mother Agnes Carriere looking for the grave of her grandmother Jemima Hall at a cemetery in Grand Rapids, Manitoba, July 20, 1994.

Photo by Ken Carriere.

My great-grandfather, Bill McKenzie. He came to Canada from the Isle of Lewis, Scotland, never to return.

Photo courtesy of Margaret Schweitzer, Denare Beach at Amisk Lake, Saskatchewan.

realizing then that death was part of life, which, coincidentally, was our beloved mosōm Dougal McKenzie's final advice to accept.

Mosōm Dougal was the centre of my mother's universe, and there were many truths he shared with his children and grandchildren, passed on from generation to generation through family oral histories. He told my mother about her paternal grandparents, Jemima Hall, originally from Oxford House, Manitoba, and William (Bill) McKenzie, who had come from the Isle of Lewis, Scotland, when he was only fifteen. My mother had always wanted to know where her father's mother was buried and was told that she had been laid to rest at Grand Rapids, Manitoba. We researched Jemima Hall's burial record, and I took Mom to Grand Rapids to visit a graveyard there. I watched with curiosity as my mother stepped softly around the graves. She had entered a sacred site and connected with her ancestors.

We also visited an elder in Grand Rapids who knew my mom's father's father and shared what he knew of him. Bill McKenzie, in addition to many other labours in his life, was once an employee of the Hudson's Bay Company and had been a commercial fisherman on Horse Island in Lake Winnipeg, where my mother's father, Dougal, had grown up. The elder also talked about Bill travelling to Churchill, on the Hudson Bay coast, where he had first arrived in Canada, had once homesteaded, and had relatives. The elder also told us that Bill was buried at The Pas. So the cemetery in Cumberland House, where we unearthed my mother's brother's remains, was a connection not only to her brother and her father but also a spiritual link beyond.

Another link to our past is a grave at the Ross Park Cemetery in Flin Flon, where my mom's stepmother, Dougal's second wife and my step-kokominaw, Christiana Cursiteur, is buried. She was a member of the Peter Ballantyne Cree Nation and related to the Rockland Cree (Nihīthawak) families who lived throughout the Churchill River (Missinipiy) country from Stanley Mission to Pelican Narrows. She became involved with the Swampy Cree (Nehinawak) when she married Dougal.

When I was in Flin Flon in the summer of 2019, I paid a visit and found that my brother Les had erected a grave marker, a stone that had taken him two summers to shape. About three years before our mother, Agnes, passed away in 2002, she requested that Les mark Christiana's burial place. As I mentioned in the introduction to this book, Christiana had taught my mother and her siblings many things that they would carry with them throughout their lives. At that pretty cemetery nestled in the rock on the southern edge of Flin Flon, I did a Cree prayer of gratitude to her spirit for giving care to Mom and her siblings.

The following is a story about life at Amisk Lake, where my mother grew up, that she shared with me. It is about the animal we call wīnask *in Cree, the groundhog in English.*

WĪNASK (GROUNDHOG)

Ēkwāni pēyakwām nikīmowānān wīnask.	*This one time we ate a groundhog.*
Tāgī otāwīyāk ēkīpiminawātigoyāk.	*Our late father cooked us this meal.*
Ēgwāni mēsci ēwītimowayāyāk	*Then just as we were to eat*
kīmōc omisi tāgī itigowāk	*slyly this is what he said,*
awa tāgī wīcisānītowāk	*this who was our sibling,*
Angus tāgītiht.	*Angus was his name.*
"Ēwako awa pisiskiw wīna	*"This here animal it*
tāmōnawāt māna cīpwaya."	*digs up human skeletons."*

Ēkwāni namwāc nikīmōwānān	*Just then we couldn't eat*

awa wīnask apisīs poko
  nikī otinānān.
	*this groundhog, only a bit
	  we took.*

Nīstanān nikīwāpātēnān ita	*We, too, we saw the place*
awa wīnask tākīwātīgēt.	*this groundhog had dug a hole.*
Ohtē anima pēyak mēgwāskān	*Over there, that one meeting place (graveyard),*
nēgwācāw mistayi mitoni wāpiskāw	*the land is very sandy, it is very white,*
anima nēgwa mistawi minwāsin.	*that sand, it is very fine.*
Māga ēgota anima tāgīwātīgēt	*That is the place where it dug a hole,*
awa wīnask.	*this groundhog.*
Ēgwāni cigēmā nitāpētawānān	*It was then for sure we really heard him,*
awa tāgītigiwāk.	*he who told us.*
"Ēwako awa tāmōnawāt cīpwaya."	*"This is the one who digs up human skeletons."*

Written by Ken Carriere June 17, 1997, based upon an oral story told by his mother, Agnes Carriere.

——◇——

While some of the Ininiwak accepted Christianity, others did not or did not fully. Many carried on with their ancestral, traditional spirituality on their reserves or in remote places away from Christian missions. My father grew up on a remote reserve and was one of those who adopted elements from the differing beliefs. He took both the Christian ways and those passed down from his elders and ancestors. As a child, he was aware of Nēhināwēwi mahimoscikēwin (the Cree way of praying), and I once heard him speaking about Cree spirituality and the practices of a respected elder at Pine Bluff, a medicine man named Sēpincēk, whose Christian name was Stephen Jake Greenleaf. My father had known Sēpincēk as a boy and spoke of him with reverence. With his older brother Alphonse, my father often went to watch Sēpincēk as he went out to do his prayers at the edge of a large muskeg. This was a sacred place to Sēpincēk, his altar to the universe where he said, in a very loud voice, his mahimoscigēwina (prayers). I have wondered if witnessing these practices took my father into Sēpincēk's spiritual realm, in which he quietly remained for the rest of his life.

My dad was close to his parents and especially his mother, and my mother once told me a story about his mother's death that spoke to his spiritual awareness of the animals in their environment. A mourning dove, which the Cree call maci pinēsīs, meaning evil bird, repeatedly visited his parents' home in Pine Bluff. His mother was having health issues, and since the bird was a bad omen, my dad kept shooting at it trying to scare it away. Following beliefs common among Indigenous Peoples, including respected elders such as Sēpincēk, my dad believed the bird was forecasting a death in his family, and he might have been right. Not long after, my grandmother Agnes Morin went to the Spirit World.

My brother John also once told me a profound story involving Sēpincēk that had to do with one of my father's stepbrother Isidore's sons, Victor. My father's stepbrother was a son from his father Leonile Carriere's first marriage. Isidore's sons would come to Pine Bluff to spend time with their grandfather Leonile; they also spent time with elders such as my mom's dad, Dougal, as well as Sēpincēk. They would go with him to tend fish nets, to hunt ducks, geese,

These photos show the war memorial, in the northern village of Cumberland House, that honours those who served and gave their lives in the First and Second World Wars.

Photos by Ken Carriere.

and moose, and to trap furbearers. They learned how to live off the land, and Sēpincēk got to know Victor well.

During the Second World War, Victor was in Europe fighting alongside the Canadian troops, and one day Sēpincēk saw an apparition of someone sitting in the bow of his canoe. It was the image of young Victor. That day Sēpincēk told someone at Pine Bluff about the apparition and said that he was worried about Victor. Not long after, a telegram was received in Cumberland House with the information that Victor was dead. In tribute to my dad's stepbrother's son, my brother John was given the middle name Victor. Killed in action on October 24, 1944, Private Victor Vernon Carriere is buried in Belgium.

My father and his brother Alphonse also served in Europe during the Second World War, but unlike Victor they survived, although my father was severely wounded on the battlefield in France. He was first taken to a field hospital; then, once strong enough, he was taken to a hospital in England. When he finally got home, my father told my mother, "Nigīpītawgok ita kāgīginēnimācik kāgīmisawganīgātīcik ostigwāniwak sīmāgansīgānak" ("They put me where soldiers had been wounded in their heads"), adding, "Ispīk kāgītiminawyāyān kāgītigiskisiyān niwīgimāgan asici nicawāsimis" ("When I got better, I remembered my wife and my child"). My dad was fortunate to make it back home to his wife on the wings of her Christian prayers, but perhaps her prayers were accompanied by the songs of Sēpincēk.

Part 2

---◇---

DROP BY, DON'T BE A STRANGER

GLEN DUBINAK INTERVIEW

$\diamond$

On March 14 and 15, 2020, I interviewed two of my cousins, brother and sister Glen Dubinak and Margaret Schweitzer, both of whom live at Denare Beach, Saskatchewan, on the northeast side of Amisk Lake. My conversations with them have a common theme. Both lived off the land like their Cree ancestors. Their mixed heritage from Eastern Europe and Scotland only shows that others have come here to join the Cree. Their legacy lives on with their Cree relatives in this northeastern part of Saskatchewan. Below is the first of these two interviews, conducted with Glen (GD), a commercial fisher, trapper, hunter, wildfire suppressor, and wild rice grower. Glen has fished commercially on Amisk Lake for most of his life.

KC: How did your family get involved in the commercial fishing at Amisk Lake?

GD: The fishing started with Grandpa Dougal when he lived with his family on Dougal's Island. They would start the fishing on December 1st. They used horses to fish out on the lake. The cabooses were tied to the horse team. The cabooses were heated by firewood. The fish were kept fresh in the caboose. They then took the fish to the railroad head at Flin Flon to get them to market.

KC: The train took the fish to Winnipeg where the market was?

GD: Yes, they did. For some reason, they had to keep the fish fresh during the winter. There was a buyer here called Booth Fisheries who handled the fish from Amisk Lake. I was told at one time that a horse fell through the ice. Everyone tried to come and help. By the time they pulled out the horse, it died. Hypothermia had set in, and the horse died. This was my dad, Mike Dubinak's, story.

KC: Where did they get the hay feed for the horses?

GD: Along the shorelines of the lakes and rivers. In the springtime, they would burn the old hay crop to make sure fresh hay would come up. Dougal even had a couple of cows at the river.

KC: By the river, you mean the Sturgeon-weir River where it flows into Amisk Lake? Northwest side of Amisk Lake?

GD: Yes, at the reserve land to Amisk Lake. For winter fishing, they went out to Dougal's Island, about 200 to 300 yards out, to set the first net.

KC: Was this about the middle part of Amisk Lake?

GD: Pretty well the middle part, it was wide open there.

KC: When the fishing started, was that in the 1930s, just when the Flin Flon mine was starting to be developed? Was it when the Mandy Mine started?[1]

GD: Yes, they hauled the ore out of there to take to Sturgeon Landing. They went down the Goose River, which flows into the Sturgeon-weir.

KC: Did they haul that ore out with horses?

GD: They used boats. They took the ore down the Sturgeon-weir River. They took the fish to Douglas Lake, where they had a fish plant. This lake is located by Creighton close to Flin Flon. Back then they used the horses to haul fish. They had to have hay and oats for the horses. That way I don't understand how they got the fresh fish to town.

KC: How did the fishers get paid?

GD: The road from Beaver Lake to Creighton had to be built. Road was fourteen miles long. The horses took the fish to the railroad yard.

KC: Someone had to put shoes on the horses.

GD: My dad put the shoes on them. I wondered if it hurt the horses.

KC: This is before trucks and cars got used in the area.

---

1   The Mandy Mine was established in 1916. It became the first productive copper mine in Manitoba. Between 1916 and 1920, over 17,000 tons of ore were transported by horse and wagon to Sturgeon Landing, then on barges to The Pas, and finally by rail to a smelter at Trail, British Columbia. Mining was briefly resumed during the Second World War.

GD: Warehouse Bay is where they had the warehouses
      on Cumberland Lake. People from Cumberland
      House came to Amisk Lake to fish for whitefish.
      The fish were taken to Cumberland House and then
      taken to The Pas for Booth Fisheries.

KC: When was Beaver City built?[2]

GD: Beaver City was built for the Gold Rush. Mom's
      story is about this fella who had been dressing fish
      all day. He saw something shiny in [the] distance. He
      decided to quit his job and to check what was going
      [on] at the location. This was towards the southwest
      side of Beaver [Amisk] Lake towards Dinner Point.
      He decided to go check what was the shiny spot.
      He never came back. When the fish plant got going
      on Amisk Lake, the summer fishing season started
      then. We had a Co-op fishery here. What happened
      to our fish plant here in Amisk Lake was when the
      Co-op Fisheries shut down and the Freshwater Fish
      Marketing Corporation [FFMC] took over. We then
      built a packhouse here.

KC: You had to haul your fish to The Pas. It got weighed
      in the Booth Fisheries plant and then put on the
      train to Winnipeg?

---

2   Beaver City was the location of Saskatchewan's first gold rush, in
     1913. Located on the south shore of Amisk Lake (see Map 4), Beaver
     City in its heyday reportedly had a federal government ranger sta-
     tion and fire tower, a Revillon Frères trading post, a boarding house,
     a Royal North-West Mounted Police post, and a ferry service. With
     the onset of the First World War, however, interest in gold waned as
     demand for copper increased significantly. By 1918, most inhabitants
     had left for nearby Flin Flon, where copper was discovered in 1915.
     Beaver City quickly became a ghost town, never to recover.

GD: A local fish buyer ended up with the packhouse here in Amisk Lake. It was sold to him for one dollar. He then ended up with the packhouse. This packhouse was built by us who at the time were part of the Co-op Fisheries. We owned it collectively. After a while, the fish buyer made a fish plant for himself. He became the agent for the Freshwater Fish Marketing Corporation. It was good for the agent and for us, the fishers.

KC: The fish plant is where you drop off your catch. Then you get a record of how much your fish weighed and the amount to expect in pay after the fish are delivered to the Freshwater Fish Market in Winnipeg, Manitoba.

GD: The local fish buyer is the agent for the FFMC. He keeps the fish fresh by putting them in plastic containers with a slurry of ice and water mix. These things are kept at a cold temperature inside the plant. Later on, they get put into a transport truck with a refrigerated unit, and it is then transported to Winnipeg.

KC: Kept fresh all the way to there.

GD: They take the fish all the way to Winnipeg from Denare Beach with the fish being totally fresh.

KC: Once they get to Winnipeg, the processing plant will prepare the fish to go onto the store counters for the customers.

GD: Yes, they do with the fish whatever they want to do with them.

KC: You are the one who produces the fish.

GD: Sometimes in the winter people want to have whitefish to eat. FFMC will buy our whitefish in the winter months.

KC: What happens to the summer fishery?

GD: During the summer months, the folks are buying hamburgers and other kinds of meat. They don't buy fish as much. During the summer months, some people destroy our nets. We shut down our fishing during the summer for those reasons. They make a mess of our nets.

KC: No respect or just ignorance when they do that.

GD: During the winter months, there isn't any tourists fishing in Amisk Lake. They no longer have their fancy boats out there to go angling from.

KC: Even with their snow machines they don't go out as much.

GD: The folks from Flin Flon and Creighton go to Maraiche Lake[3] to go fishing for pickerel. That's the most popular place around here.

KC: Do some of them go fishing at Mari Lake?[4]

---

3   Maraiche Lake is a large lake just east of the south end of Amisk Lake (see Map 4).

4   Mari Lake is a very long lake running north-south. The southern end is roughly twenty kilometres north of Flin Flon in Saskatchewan.

GD: Some go there, but I'm the only one with a commercial fishing licence for Mari Lake.

KC: Do they have a limit for the angling fisher?

GD: Daily limit is three pickerel in Manitoba and four in Saskatchewan.

KC: So the people spend a lot of money on winter ice fishing?

GD: One guy I met at the gas station told me that he went out to the river [the mouth of Sturgeon-weir into Amisk Lake] to do some ice fishing. He caught three pickerel there. He spent forty-seven dollars on gasoline to go there and back. The company workers make all the money. They buy all the toys: new machines, snow machines, quads, snow trackers, ice shacks with all the amenities—TV, sleeping quarters, etc. When they get days off, they go out there and even stay out there. Fish all day if they want.

KC: That way they can beat the system of catch limits. Stay out there all day. Cook your fish for ice shack lunch. Bring home the legal limit for the day.

GD: Logging roads go into Maraiche Lake. There was a petition put out by Flin Flon, Manitoba, anglers to allow them to go into Maraiche Lake, which is totally in Saskatchewan.

KC: Government of Saskatchewan allows it to happen.

GD: Flin Flon anglers got away with it by signed petition. Sorry to hear that this happened. George Cursiteur [pronounced Custer] was the last commercial fisher from Denare Beach to be licensed to commercial fish at Maraiche Lake. He got shut down because the anglers from Flin Flon, Manitoba, signed the petition to shut down the commercial fishery at Maraiche Lake. This was allowed to happen by the Saskatchewan government.

KC: That was wrong, a gross injustice.

GD: It was wrong.

KC: They shut down a First Nations fisher and his livelihood. He could thank Saskatchewan's Flin Flon Extensions of Boundary Act, 1952. Flin Flon anglers no doubt used it to their advantage.

GD: His wife, Christina, is still alive in her eighties. Lives here on the reserve. George died out there on the land. He worked on fire crew. He quit fire crew to go line cutting. He carried on with commercial fishing on Beaver Lake. Fished on Amisk Lake, too, like us. Harold, his son, took over.

KC: Seems hard to keep it going, then, from one generation to the other.

GD: It's a bit like that. George was a fisher. When he couldn't commercial fish at Maraiche Lake anymore, he tried another lake nearby in Saskatchewan where he caught big jackfish.

KC: Did he take tourists over there too?

GD: No, another person ran the tourist operation. He hired local guides. There's only one buyer for fish, that is the FFMC. It's getting harder to make a living at commercial fishing.

KC: So you can't really sell your fish locally as the holder of a commercial fishing licence. Like the commercial fishers do where I live, at Lac La Ronge.

GD: You can go to the local fish plant owner here to buy pickerel fillets. As the agent for FFMC out of Winnipeg, he has to buy those fish from FFMC— then he can sell those bought fish locally. Ten pounds of pickerel fillets from the local owner sells at a hundred and forty dollars.

KC: How does that work?

GD: If the local fish plant owner buys pickerel for FFMC, he pays me three dollars a pound. He then buys those same fish from FFMC at a set price. Then he turns around and sets his own price for the fish he bought from FFMC. During the summer months, the local fish plant owner operates a packing plant at Pelican Narrows.

KC: How many workers does he hire?

GD: He hires two workers to operate the pack house. He pays by hourly wage about five workers to come in to make pickerel fillets. When the pack house has enough fish ready for pickup, he will drive his refrigerated truck to Pelican Narrows to pick up the prepared fish. He brings them back to his fish plant and gets them ready to move them to FFMC in Winnipeg. Right now this local fish plant owner here in Denare Beach is going to Buffalo Narrows to bring fish for his fish plant, mostly jackfish. He tried to buy fish from Reindeer Lake, but there's too many pounds of fish there—over a million pounds. His operation couldn't handle that much. In Pelican Narrows and other tourist lodge operations during July and August, these have changed a lot. In the old days, most tourists would book in and come by air flight. Nowadays the tourists come in large groups by motor home. They bring their own boats and motors. Everything right down to toilet paper. There's not much there for the tourist lodge operator. The local Denare Beach tourist operator, he only rents out cabins now. The tourists will come with their own boat and motor with fishing gear. They will not rent his boats nor motor[s]; they bring their own. He can charge so much for renting his cabin. He won't hire guides for the tourists. Tourists go on their own. He used to have a motel, but the motel rooms don't get rented out. Most tourists will stay in his cabins, and some will stay in their motor homes. They will come as a large group, let's say six in the group. He will charge twelve hundred bucks for a weekend for the cabin rental. Those tourists will pay two hundred dollars each person for the entire weekend. That's cheap.

KC: So locals don't make that much money anymore from the tourist trade.

GD: I know of one group that came from Kansas State, USA, mostly farmers. They bring their own food prepackaged—huge beef steaks frozen and ready for grilling. They come in from Winnipeg towards Thompson, then come through Snow Lake. Less than two days to come from Kansas State. They don't come through The Pas at all.

Left to right: Glen's father Mike Dubinak (my uncle), with Glen's older brothers John and Howard, with their truck for hauling fish and equipment.

Photo courtesy of the Dubinak family collection, Denare Beach, Saskatchewan.

KC: When you talk about commercial fishing in Amisk Lake, you can't do much of that anymore in this lake?

GD: We only winter commercial fish in March when the weather is better. We shut down during July and August. That's when anglers come in from all over to fish in Amisk Lake.

KC: In terms of Amisk Lake itself—a place that had good commercial fishing—it no longer has the same capacity it once had. Maybe a depletion in the resource.

GD: The fish have an economic value. A tub of jackfish at sixty pounds is only worth forty dollars. Depending on the size of the fish species, you will be paid more. If the fishing is good, you need to catch twenty tubs of fish.

KC: Do you use fish finders?

GD: I know the lake well enough to go where the best spots are for catching different kinds of fish—from pickerel, [to] whitefish, to jackfish.

KC: So you have what is called traditional knowledge. Something you got from way back passed on through the generations.

GD: I started fishing with my dad when I was twelve years old. I am now seventy-four years old and still commercial fishing on Amisk Lake.

KC: Where did you go to school? Did you finish high school? And where did you go study after finishing high school?

GD: I went to school in Saskatoon, where I took the courses in conservation officer training. I was supposed to get work in Manitoba, but I took a job in Saskatchewan instead.

KC: So, in fact, you never gave up on commercial fishing. You have been doing this all of your life.

Mike Dubinak's son John (left) and his helper Chris Norman holding up Mike's record lake trout caught in Amisk Lake.

Photo courtesy of the Dubinak family collection, Denare Beach, Saskatchewan.

GD: There's never been a winter I haven't commercial
fished in Amisk Lake since I was twelve years old.
We weren't paid that much for our fish back in
the old days.

KC: So how did you survive?

GD: In the summer months, we stayed out at the cabin
on Amisk Lake. We had a garden where we grew
veggies. We had oatmeal for breakfast. Then we had
fish for lunch with salad from the garden. Then we
had fish for supper with potatoes from our garden.

MARGARET SCHWEITZER INTERVIEW

◇

The following interview conducted on March 15, 2020, was with Glen Dubinak's sister, Margaret Schweitzer, my cousin, who also lives at Denare Beach, Saskatchewan. In our conversation, Margaret (MS) also spoke of traditions passed down through the generations.

KC: Tell me how it was like growing up with your family on Amisk Lake.

MS: I grew up with my brother Glen; we were close in age. We went out on Amisk Lake with our parents when they did their commercial fishing. When we were very young, we had to scrub the fish boxes. We got to know Hayes Island from one end to the other.[1] We got to build tree houses. During the winter, we built snow shelters with spruce boughs.

---

1   Hayes Island is located in the west-central part of Amisk Lake (see Map 4).

Lots of stuff like that. When we got older, Glen, me, and Mom would go in a canoe to go pick berries. Later on, Dad would take us to the river. There we would visit some sites and stop in to visit people.

KC: When you say river, is that the Sturgeon-weir?

MS: Yes. That's the west Weir. The river flows from the Churchill River and north from Reindeer Lake. When it floods at the Frog Portage, it then flows out this way.[2] We then know we will get high water on Amisk Lake. It goes eventually down to Sturgeon Landing and Cumberland House. Hayes Island is south of Dougal's Island—Grandpa's island—west of there is Muskeg Bay, then south of there is Dinner Point, just west of there is the river. People still use that place a lot. They moved into Indian Island right beside Missi Island.[3]

KC: Why call it Indian Island?

MS: They came there from the river to work at the fish-packing plant. They were not allowed to camp by where the beach is. They had to stay on the island.

---

2   The Sturgeon-weir River has its headwaters near the community of Pelican Narrows. Frog Portage was a vital link between the Saskatchewan River and Churchill River systems during the fur trade era and is still used by canoeists.

3   Missi Island is a large island in the northern section of Amisk Lake (see Map 4). The name Missi is an English abbreviation of the Cree word missiministik, meaning big island. Travelling around Missi Island by canoe takes about two or three days for a single paddler or about one or two days for two paddlers. It is a trip of approximately fifty kilometres.

This is the birchbark basket that Margaret showed me. It is a definite keepsake of hers, and it holds many memories of her nephews and nieces who came to visit her. She called it "the crayon basket." In it, she kept a good supply of pencils and crayons for the youngsters to draw and sketch. With great pride, she estimated that the basket is at least eighty years old. It is still in very good condition.

Photo by Ken Carriere.

KC: Did you ever hear about a woman named Nancy Thomas? Nancy was a midwife among other things she was famous for.

MS: No. You see this basket, it is over eighty years old. My older brother John died when he was eighty years old. Unfortunately, my brother Howard died in 1976 in a hunting accident at twenty-seven years of age.[4] Howard always smiled even when working on highway projects. He enjoyed everything he did. He had a beaded buckskin jacket; my nephew Jody has it in PA. I took that jacket with me to New Zealand when I went to visit Aunt Lizzy. Boarded a ship in Vancouver. *Daily Reminder*, a newspaper printed in Flin Flon, should have a copy of that tragic story. On February 7th is when he was killed. I had to come home from New Zealand to be there for Howard's funeral.

KC: My uncle Bill Carriere had a lead dog that helped him win the World Championship Dog Race at The

---

4   This tragedy happened when Margaret's father, Mike Dubinak, accidentally shot his son Howard while they were hunting.

My uncle, Bill Carriere, kneeling (centre) with his Inuit-bred lead dog and the Northern Manitoba Trappers' Festival "Fur Queen" after winning the World Championship Dog Race in The Pas in 1961. My father, Pierre Carriere, is looking on, standing behind Miss Thompson's right shoulder.

Photo from the Ron Mackay Collection, Northern Saskatchewan Archives, La Ronge, Saskatchewan.

Pas. My brother John said it was an Inuit breed of sled dog. It may have been brought to Cumberland House by Great-Grandfather Bill McKenzie.[5]

MS: I went up to Neultin Lake Lodge in northern Manitoba and NWT.[6] Owner was a white man. I can't remember his name. He had six puppies, wanted to get rid of them. I brought the pups home.

---

5   William "Bill" McKenzie was my maternal great-grandfather. See the chapter "Where Prayers Are Called Upon."

6   Neultin Lake straddles the border between Manitoba and Nunavut.

Uncle Bill Carriere showed up and wanted the dogs. I gave him the pups. He took them.

KC: When was this, in the late fifties or early sixties?

MS: In the sixties.

KC: In 1961, Bill won the Championship Dog Race at The Pas. His lead dog must have been about five years old.

MS: I would think so.

KC: Old Bill McKenzie took two separate trips to Fort Churchill on the coast of Hudson Bay.

MS: He took the trips to Fort Churchill through Amisk Lake from Cumberland House. He took two separate trips like that. He would go up to the Churchill River following the lakes and rivers up the Sturgeon-weir to Pelican Narrows, then to Frog Portage. Once on the Churchill River, he followed the river route down to Hudson Bay and Port of Churchill in Manitoba. Everyone was simply amazed that he did the trip twice.

KC: He must have been very athletic. He was born in the Isle of Lewis, Outer Hebrides of Scotland.

MS: I went to visit the Isle of Lewis in Scotland. I met one of his cousins. I went to Churchill, Manitoba, with Mom and Dad. We went on a tugboat to the mouth of the Churchill River. We saw where Great-Grandpa Bill McKenzie had his homestead. Dad had relatives in Churchill. They were from Winnipegosis.

KC: Bill's wife was Jemima Hall. She was from Oxford House.

MS: Yes, she was from there.

KC: Aunt Mary [McKenzie] Warren, Bill and Jemima's daughter, was the one who told about her mother.

MS: Did you ever hear how Aunt Mary ended up living with your mom and dad?

KC: No, I was away to school when she arrived.

MS: Well, when that awful hunting accident happened, Glen decided to move back home from Saskatoon. He didn't want Dad to be alone on the land. He was already married with Judy. When he arrived, Aunt Mary was going to lose her room. Your mom and dad decided she could come and live with them in Cumberland House. One thing about Aunt Mary was she loved meat. I took her out for supper at a restaurant in Nipawin for her ninety-ninth birthday. When we arrived, the whole town of Cumberland showed up. I told her she could have anything in the menu which had meat. She told me that, when she stayed at the old folks home, they used to feed her meat mashed up like a hamburger. This was awful to her. She wanted real meat. She ordered two pork chops for her dinner. She could only eat one. She wanted to take the other home to have it later.

KC: She tried to keep independent as long as she could. Had she gone to residential school in Selkirk, Manitoba?

MS: Yes, she did.

My mother, Agnes Carriere, with her niece Margaret Schweitzer at Margaret's home in Denare Beach, Amisk Lake, Saskatchewan.

Photo by Ken Carriere.

KC: My mom told me a story about Aunt Mary, who wasn't sure what race of people she was. She had always thought of herself as being Caucasian. The fact that her skin colour was brown did not enter her mind. One day she told my mom that she was a white lady. My mom approached her to tell her "Well, Auntie, if you are a white woman, I must be a white woman too." They both had a good laugh about that. My mom was an Indian woman with the greatest of pride. Where you stayed as a family during the commercial fishing on Amisk Lake, just let me know that once again please.

MS: Our island was directly west of Dougal's Island. We lived at Hayes Island.

KC: Is the Hayes Island where your dad grew potatoes?

MS: The island is at the mouth of the Sturgeon-weir River. My dad never turned anyone away. Always gave them a place to stay at our home in Creighton.

FRANKLIN COTTER CARRIERE INTERVIEW

◇

The following conversation was with my older brother Franklin Cotter Carriere (FC) and took place in La Ronge, Saskatchewan, on March 8, 2020. I recorded our talk in our Swampy Cree and later wrote it down and made an English translation. Franklin was born on October 27, 1945, to our father, Pierre (Chi Pierre) Carriere Sr., and his wife, our mother, Nora Agnes Carriere (née McKenzie), nine months after our father had returned home following his near-fatal injury in Europe during the Second World War. As I mentioned in the chapter "Of Wetigos and War," Franklin's first name honours Frank Chaboyer, the man who saved our father's life on the battlefield when Dad was left for dead. My brother's middle name, Cotter, pays respect to our dad's childhood friend George Cotter, a navy veteran of the war, at whose home our father had learned to play piano when he was young.

When our father resumed his trapping and commercial fishing after the war, Franklin would accompany him as a child. After Dad began an outfitting venture for paying customers, Franklin became his helper at age fourteen. Today Franklin still gets out on the land.

We began our conversation discussing an enormous sturgeon our father once caught.

KC: Ēwago ana kāgī-ācimat schoolteacher ēgīpētagosīk kapēcigāstēpitāt anigi mistinamewa kitāwīnaw kāgīgācitināt. Ēgwāni gīpēcigāstēpicigēw.

Your story about a schoolteacher who came to take pictures of the big sturgeon that Dad caught in a net. It was then she took pictures.

FC: Mīcēcīs ana kāgīhotināk. Anigi gotagak nāpēwak wīstawāw ēgīnōtēcigāstepicīcik. "Proof is there." Anima ēgosi ēgītōtāgwāk. Ēwago ētigwē mawatēs ēmisigitit namēwak. Nīsta anis nigīpagitawān namēwak oci. Mīcēt anigi forty- to sixty-pounders nigīgācitinānānak, anigi asici ten, twenty, twenty-five pounders ēgwani mīna mīcēt nigīgācitinānānak. Māga anigi kāmisigiticik namēwak ēgwani mōna mwāsik nigīgācitinānānak.

There was a few she took. Them other men, they, too, wanted to have their picture taken. "Proof is there." This is what she did for us. I think that was the biggest of the sturgeons. I was a fisher, too, for sturgeon. There were many forty to sixty pounders that we caught; there were also ten, twenty, twenty-five pounders. We caught many of those. But the biggest sturgeon, those ones we seldom caught.

[In English only] The fisheries was in the northwest part of Cumberland Lake. Used both hooks and nets. Would catch the sturgeon in nets in the swift-running water. This is where the sturgeon swam, their feeding grounds. Fished near the three rocky islands and camped at Oldman's Island. Would set nets at night, then got up early in the morning to check the nets. That way most of the sturgeon would still be in the nets. The fish could easily get loose from the nets. They are powerful swimmers. It would not take long for them to get free.

KC: Tānēgi oci?

Why is that?

FC: Kāmisigiticik mistahi sōgipicigēwak mōna niwēcigācitinānānak. Gītagwātagāwak osāmi pogo ēpimāpagocik ēgwa gisik ēgosīsi ēmīcisocik. Ita kāgīpagitawāyāk gisiwak miniscigosa ita māna kāgīhasayigēyāk sīsīpak oci.

The big ones were powerful pullers, they weren't easy to catch. They swam in usually with the current flow, and they would eat along the way. Where we fished was near the island where we hunted ducks.

KC: Ēgīpāwistigoyāk ēgota?

A rapids occurred there?

FC: Mōna mitoni māga kīgisīciwasin ēgota gēciwak. Oldman's Island gītamak anima ministik. Ēgota gēciwak kāgīpagitawēyāk. Ētipiskāk mānà kāgīpagitawāyāk. Kīspin namwāc wīpac kinātanapān asay kigagēcigōwak anigi namewak. Gaskītāwak kagēcigōcik anis ēsōgipicigēcik.

It was not really such a fast current there. They called it Oldman's Island, that one island. We set our

FACING PAGE: Pierre Carriere (right), showing off the 160-pound sturgeon he caught on the Central Angling River, with his sons (from left to right) Clifford, Kenneth (me), and Franklin.

When my dad brought the sturgeon into the fish weigh station at the Bigstone River Landing at Cumberland House, my brother Franklin was working as the weigh master. Recognizing that the sturgeon was possibly the biggest caught that season, Franklin thought a photo should be taken. He went to get one of the teachers from the local school, Anne Nesbitt, originally from Prince Albert, since he knew she had a camera. With Clifford and me in tow, we all headed down to the Bigstone River Landing for the photo shoot.

Many years later my other brother, Les, met a man named Don Hunter, who happened to be married to the teacher, now Mrs. Anne Hunter. While Les was visiting the Hunters one day in Prince Albert, Anne shared some of her photos of her earlier experiences in Cumberland House, and there was this photo.

Photo by Anne Hunter (née Nesbitt) of Prince Albert, courtesy of Les Carriere, Cumberland House.

> *nets close to there. We would set our nets at nightfall. If you didn't go check your nets early, the sturgeon would get off your net. They could get off the net; they were powerful pullers.*

KC: Tānsi kāgītagōcimayēgok anigi anapiyak?

How did you set the nets?

FC: Ita mwātēs ēgisīciwak ēgota kāgī agōcimāgok anigi anapiyak. Ēgota anigi namewak ēpēpagamāpagocik kisīciwan anis anima sīpī. Māgīna part of the Saskatchewan River ocitāw pogo kagisīciwāk. Ēgwa ēgota mistasinī nitāgopitānān māmihk ita kātagōcīk anapiy. Ēgwa ispik kāpēnātanapēyāk wīpac kāpētāpāk āsay māna anapiy kāgwēskāpagot. Sēmāk nigīgiskēnītēnān misāgamik ēgīgācitināgok. Ēgwa gēskaw kāgīgēcigonāgok.

Where the current is the greatest is where we set the nets. There those sturgeon would get pulled in by the current; it has a very strong one, that river. It is part of the Saskatchewan River; it has a strong current. Then there, a big rock we tied, downstream where it floats the net. And when we check the net early, by daybreak, already usually the net was straightened out. Right away we knew many were caught. Then quickly we took them off the net.

KC: Namōna na cīstapānātik kigīyāpaciyāwāw?

You didn't use an anchor pole?

FC: Tāpwē ēgota ṅigīgitāwatawānān pēyak cīstapānātik natimihk isi ēgwa mistasinī māmihk wīna kāgīyagōcimāyāk. Ispīk ēpētagopaniyak kāgisēpak mitoni gīgwēskagōcin anapiy.

Sure, there we drove in one anchor pole upstream side, and a big rock downstream side we dropped in the water. When we came to check the net in the morning, the net had floated straight.

KC: Ayō gotak ācimowin kānōtē pētātān kayācimostawiyan. Ispīk māna kāgīsopētēyēk kanitewanīgēyēk. Migiskāw ēwago isinīgātamak ēgota na māna kāgītisopwētēyāk?

And another story I would like to hear from you. Tell me about the trapping you did just around freeze-up (migiskāw). That's when you would leave to go trapping.

FC: Ēh, ēh ēgota māna kāgīsopwēwotēwāk. Nistam ita kāgīgipīcīyāk Jim's Camp gīsinīgātēw. Ita

anima kāgēskiciwak anima sipiy. Ēgwāni ēgota
oci nigītōtēwnān anima ita Angling River.
Kāwaskiciwāk ēgwa ita Grassberry River
kāpēsāgēciwāk. Ēgota kāgīpēwak iskok kigayāgatik.
Ēgota kāgīsēsawi pātācik nitēminānak. Pitamā
kasēsāwicik pāmawēsk kigamāci otāpayāgok, Ēgwa
ēgota oci kāgīsopwētēyāk ita kāgēskipimiciwak
sipiy Cumberland Lake katīsiciwak. Ēgwāni anitē
Pine Bluff kātitagosiniyak. Ēgwāni ēgota oci kānte
sopwēwotēwak. Asay ēgospīk ēti mēskanāgēyāk.
Ēgwa mīna piyātak nigīpimōtēwonān māga anis
kiyāpic ēpapagwatik.

*Yes, it was then we usually went on our trip. The first
place we stopped was Jim's Camp, it was called. It is
where the current makes a turn on that river. Then
from there we travelled to where the Angling River
is. That river then runs off the side, and it is where
the Grassberry River comes out. We stayed here long
enough to wait for the freeze-up. It is where they
could run to exercise our dogs. It is now they exercise
before we start driving them. And then from there we
left on the turning river that flows to Cumberland
Lake. And there at Pine Bluff we arrived. And then it
was from there we would travel out. It was then we
made trail. Then, too, carefully we travelled because
it is thin, the ice surface.*

KC: Tānite ōgi atimwak kāpimpātācik cīgi sīpihk?

*Where did those dogs run, along the shore of
the river?*

FC: Ēhotāpāstimēyāk āsay nigīskēnītēnān ita kapāstēk
asici ita kāgīsiciwāk sīpiy. Ēgwa mīna pāmawēsk

kāwīyāsiwamāk sīpiy nigīgocītānān inigok
kāspītatik.

*We were driving dogs then. We knew where it was
dry ground and where the river had a fast current.
And also before we were to cross a river, we checked
the ice thickness.*

KC: Kēgwān kāgīyapacītāyēk cīgahigan na?

What did you use, an axe?

FC: Pogo kēgwan gīyapacitāw.

He [Dad] used anything.

KC: Mīcigiw maga?

What about an ice checker?

FC: Osāmi pogo mistik gīyapacitāw. Ēgīcīpogayak
kīspin sāpoyēpinam anima mistik ēgwāni osām
papagatin. Ēgwa mīna cīgahigan oci kīspin nāntaw
two to three inches isi gispagatin ēgwāni asay
nigiyāswayēnān. Kāginaw kēgwān nigīpimotatānān;
pagwānigamik, kotawānapisk, nitagōpināna, sōswāc
kāginaw kēgwān.

*Mostly, he used a stick. He cut a pointed end. If he
pushed that stick through the ice, it was not thick
enough. And with an axe, if the ice was two to three
inches thick, then we crossed over on that ice. We
carried everything: a tent, a stove, our blankets—
it was everything.*

KC: Tāntowak anigi otāpānāskwak kāgīyāpaciyayēgok?

What kind of sleighs did you use?

FC: Freight Alaska sleighs anigi. Nahīnigok anigi kīkinosiwak.

They were called Alaska sleighs mostly used for carrying freight.

KC: Otānāk kinīpawin ēgwa ēgota astēw kamicimīyan?

Did you stand on the back of the sleigh's runners and hold on to the sleigh's handlebars?

FC: Otānāk isi kīginosiw ēgota kinīpawin ēgwa kimicimīn mistik. Ēgwa mīna kināgiyēpiskawāw kawīciyacik anigi atimwak. Kīminopanin ana. Ēgwāni māna kawēsk nigīyatoskānān kapimōtēwāk. Mōna mīna wānaw nigītohtēwnān kāpipohk ōma mōna konesk kīsigāstēw. Sēmāk kapētāpāk kāgīwanskāt Kisēyiniw Dad. Ēgwāni gētskaw kāgīgisēpāyi mīcsosiyāk. Āsay mīna gitwām kātisopwē ōtēwāk kātimēskanāgēyāk. Māgīna three to four hours pogo ēgīsigāk. Tāpwē pogo ētimeskanāgēyāk mōna wānaw nigītohtēwnān. Anta oci Pine Bluff kāsopwēwōtēwāk ēgwāni nētē kāpimitatinahk iskok pīnisk kāgītagosiniyak. Ēgota anima ēpimāskēyahk isinīgātēw. Tāgōtatin anima ēgota kāgīgospicisayigēyāk. Ēgota anima mistimaskēk kāgotītamak. Mōna mīna pogowīta ana Kisēyiniw gīocigapēsiw. Pogo kamītisiskānik mistahi kinagacītāw.

In the back, it was longer where you stood, and you held on to the wood. And, too, we pushed with our legs to help the dogs. It went well, that thing. We worked hard when we travelled. Not that far we could travel during winter; then it was not daylight that long. As soon as daybreak came, he got up, the old man, Dad. We quickly had breakfast. Then we started out again; then we broke trail. Because then it was three to four hours only for daylight. For sure we had to break trail and couldn't travel very far. After leaving Pine Bluff, a place they call kāpimitatinahk (rising rock ridge), there we finally got to. There where is kāpimāskēyāk (a wooded ridge), it is called. On that ridge is where we drove our dogs. It is where we came onto a huge muskeg. It was not just anyplace that the old man camped. It had to have a good supply of firewood.

KC: Tānitowak mihta kāgīnatonāk?

What kind of wood was most preferred?

FC: Ēpāstēnigi minahikwak oci.

It was dry spruce wood.

KC: Nīpisītagwa māga?

Did he pick dried willows?

FC: Pogīyitowak tēpināk ēpāstenigi.

He picked whatever was dry.

KC: Tānsi ana ogotawānāpisk kāgīyāwāwek?

How was it, the stove you had?

FC: Kīminosiw ana ēgota giyastēw ita kapiminawāsoyan. Nēwo giyastēwa pāskītēnigana. Ēgwatowak kotawanāpisk kawēsk nanāto kagītīgasāwān. Inato cooking stove.

It was good. It even had an oven for cooking. It had four openings. That kind of stove where you can cook any kind of meal. It was a real cooking stove.

KC: Bannock mīna ēgota kāgīpiminawāson?

Did he cook bannock in the oven?

FC: Pogīkēgwān kagīpiminawason. Ēgosi mīna gītwēw "kīspin namwāc kigēcināwon ēminawāsik wiyās. Kawosaman pogo kawēsk ēgwa gītwām kitisāsāpiskisēn."

You can cook all kinds of meals. He also said, "If you are not sure the meat is good, boil it until it is well done, and then you fry it."

KC: Kītwam kasāsāpiskisaman?

So he fried it afterwards?

FC: Ēh, ēh ēgosi anima, kīminēnītam ēsāsāpiskisigēt.

Yes, that's it. He loved frying meat.

KC: Kēgo pimiy kagiyāpacītāt kasāsāpiskisigēt?

What did he use for frying meat?

FC: Lard, everything lard. Māgīnigok kāgīsītatoskēyak. Mitoni sēmāk nigīwanīgasenān anima lard.

*He used lard, everything lard. Since we worked
physically hard, we quickly burned the lard out.*

KC: Semāk egīwanīgasamek?

You quickly burned it out?

FC: Tāpwē nigiyāpwēsīskāgonān anima. Inigok
kātoskēyāk nigīmistiyapwēsinān. Mōna
nigīmisigitin ēgwaspīk. Ēgwa wīsta osām pogo
pēgwan kīspīcinigwatiw. Nāntaw 150 pounds
nigīspīcinigwatin. Nīna māna kāgīnīgānipātāyān.
Atimwak ēpimicisawocik. Ēgwa wīna
ēwotāpāstimēt.

*It sure made us sweat, that. The amount we worked,
we sweated a lot. I wasn't big then.. Then him too,
he weighed about the same. Around 150 pounds I
weighed. Me, I usually ran ahead. The dogs would
follow me. Then he would drive the dogs.*

KC: Asāmak ēgiskawacik?

Did you wear snowshoes?

FC: Namwāc ēmoscipātāyān pāgwēginaskisina pogo
egiskamān.

No, I ran with my moccasins only.

KC: Ēgispagāk kēgwin ēgiskaman?

A thick hide you wore?

FC: Ita mwātēs kagispagāk pāgwēgin mōna
sēmāk kipīgowēpiskēn. Kīminwāsina anigi

pāgwēginaskisina. Mistahi gītagāgi osīcigātēwa.
Kīminosītāw ana kimāmānaw maskisina. Canvas
tops mīna ēgiyastāt ēgwa namwāc sēmāk
kasāpwāpēyan mistahi gīminwāsina.

*Where the hide is the thickest, not right away you
wear it out. They were really good, those moccasins.
They were well made. Our mom had made them to
perfection. She used a heavy canvas to make the tops.
She knew how to make moccasins for working outside
in the snow. The moosehide at the bottom part was
very thick. It did not break up right away. We didn't
get wet feet wearing them. They were well made.*

KC: Tānita mwātēs ēgispagāk pāgwēgin ana mōswa
kāpāgwonat ispīk?

What part of the moose is the hide the thickest?

FC: Ita mwātēs kāsōgisit anta nīgān kāwocigāpawit.
Māgīna anigi yāpēwak kāyisiwēpawawtocik.
Ocitaw pogo kagispagānigi osagayāwa. Nāntaw
half inch inigok isi gispagāw ēgota pāgwēgin.
Kawēpawawtocik anigi mōna gīsāpowēpāmak
inigok ēgota ēgispagāk anima pāgwēgin.
Misinōtintowak anigi māna ispik kanōtintocik.
Mīcētwāw nigīnatotawānānak ēmatēnōtintocik.
Āskaw nigīkanawāpamānānak ēnōtintocik. Mōna
nigīgēsēgiyānānak papiyātak nigīpimāgamigisinān.
Ayāw mīna mōna pogowispik nigīgēnipānān
mōswa. Ispīk kanatayēnītamāk wiyās ēgota māna
kāgīnipawāyāk mōswa.

*Where the moose is the strongest built, in the front
where it stands, for sure. Just the way those bulls
use their antlers, they certainly need to have a thick*

hide. It is about a half inch thick there, that skin.
When they are hit with the antlers, it couldn't break
through, it is so thick there, that hide. They fight
each other hard when they fight. Many times we
heard them fight one another. Sometimes we saw
them fighting. We did not try to scare them off. We
went about quietly doing our work. And then, too, at
just any time, we didn't kill a moose—only when we
needed the meat, then we killed a moose.

KC: Mōna mīna pogītowak gīnipayēw?

What kind of moose did you kill? Did you kill the
yearlings?

FC: Ēh ēh anigi kāpisīsicik ēgwni māna kāgīnipawāgīcik.
Nāntaw anigi nīswāw egwa nistwāw askīnecik
egwāni kāgīnatawēnimāgok. Āpisci cēskanēsiwak
ēgwani. Gīwinowak ēgwani namwāc anis
wīnawāw mistahi ēgīpāmpātācik. Kītapasiwak
mīna kagēnōtinigēcik. Gīsāgōtāpinatāwak anis
mistiyāpēwak anigi gīnociyigowak pogo ēgītapasīcik.

Yes, the smaller moose are the ones we killed. Mostly
the ones who were three years old; those are the ones
we wanted. Small antlered, those ones. These ones
were usually fat; they had not been running around.
They ran away rather than fight. They were badly
beaten; since the big bulls beat them up, they had
to run away.

KC: Ēgwāni ocitaw ōma nōcimihk kāwītāgamigisiyan.

I suppose you need to know how to live well out
in the bush.

FC: Tāpwē ēgwāni ēwako pogo kanagacīsiyan oma nōcimihk kawītāgamigisiyan.

Yes, you need to know how to live out there in the bush.

Osāmpogo anigi nēwo egwa niyānan otēskaniyāwa kācīpwānigi ēgwani māna gīwīnosiyak. Anigi mistiyāpēwak wīnawāw na gīpāwaniyak. Ēgwāni inigok mistahi ēgīpāmpātācik. Mīcētwaw nigīpētawānānak ēmategāgitocik. Awsascīna kānawāstik ēgospīk kiggātāgosiwak. Ēgwāni mitoni gisiwāk nigīpēcimānānak. Ēgwa oci osām wānaw Kigayitowatēyāk.

It was usually those ones with two and five antler points, those ones were nicely fat. Those big bulls, they were quite skinny. That's because they had been running around. Many times we heard them calling. Especially when it was calm, they were loud. It was then we called them to us real close. That way, too, not so far we had to carry the meat.

Tōstōskamin anis ōma Cumberland mistahi kigatoskan wānaw kayitowatēyan mōsopwāma. Tōstōskiwan Cumberland, it's a bog. Ana wīna mistiyāpēw gaskitāw kapimpātāt ita kātōstōskāk. Anis wīna osita ētasēgānigi. Kiyām āta inigok ēmisigitit ēgwa ēgasigatit kiyāpic gaskitāw kasōgānēpātāt ēgota. Sōgānēwiyāmo māna kātapasīgoyāk. Nāntaw 800 to 1,000 pounds ispīcinigatiw.

It is a bog there at Cumberland; you will work hard to carry a hind quarter. It is boggy, Cumberland. That big bull moose, he can run in the boggy ground.

After a moose hunt (left to right): my adopted brother Joe McKay, Don Bird, Brian Hoffard, and Franklin Carriere. Franklin and the seven other hunters on this trip each got a moose after eight days of hunting. Think of the power of eight for this moose hunt.

Photo courtesy of Franklin Carriere, La Ronge, Saskatchewan.

> *It has a split hoof. Never mind how big it is, and how heavy it is, he can still run fast there. He runs away so fast when it runs from us. He weighs from 800 to 1,000 pounds.*

KC: Gasigwatiw ēsa?

It is heavy, then?

FC: Nigīgitowānānak anigi yāpēwak kapēcimāgok. Mitoni gisiwahk kāpēcimāgok pāmawēsk kapāskisowāgok kanīpēgawsowāk. Tāpwē anima ēgwa kigīgiskēnītēn inigok ēgwasigaticik kayāwatāyan wiyās nohcimihk ohci. Ēgwāni

160

ita kāgīgawayāyāk ana yāpēw. Nēwowayik
māna isi kāgītāskisawāyāk. Ēgwa ēgota oci
kāgīpostowatēwayāk. Ita māna kāgīnipawayāk
namwac māna pēyakwāw nigīwocipagitināw. Āsay
ēgospīk ēgīsōgowatēyān.

*We called the bulls to come to us. We wanted them
to come really close before we shot to kill them. True
that is and you knew how heavy they were when
you carried their meat out of the bush. Then where
we felled that bull. Into four parts we usually cut
it. Then we would put the parts on each other for
carrying. From where we killed it I never once put it
down. At that time, I could carry heavy loads.[1]*

KC: Āsay ēgīsōgowatēyan ēgospīk? Mōna ēsa piyātak
kigītāgamigisināwāw.

*So you already could carry heavy weights? You didn't
just do things quietly.*

FC: Mistahi āsay nigīsōgowatān māgina inigok
ēgīgasigwāgi kāginaw kēgwān katasīgamāk. Āpō
anigi twenty-foot freighters kagiyāpacitāyāk mōna
piyātak gigasigwana. Ocitaw pogo kagaskwēwatēyan
kāginaw kēgwān kapētowatatāyan.
Nigīmaskwacisinān ōma kāgītāgamigisiyāk.
Misiwēyita ēgīmoscipimiskāyāk. Mēstas anima
Kisēyiniw kāgīgaskinēyāk pīwāpiskos ēgwa ēgota
kāgīsopwēpaniyāk. Eight-horse Johnson gīhayāw
āpōcigwa ēwago gīgasigwan.

---

1   My brother Franklin was bragging about his packing power. His
claim to fame is that he once carried 1,225 pounds of flour in a flour-
packing contest at the Meadow Lake Winter Festival, showing off to
the cowboys there. He still holds the record for the packing event.

I already was able to carry heavy weights. I was doing heavy work all the time. We used twenty-foot freighter canvas canoes for work. I already carried heavy canoes when I did a portage. I was always exercising. We paddled everywhere we went. We didn't have an outboard motor yet. It was later that Dad was able to afford the outboard. He had an eight-horsepower Johnson. It was a heavy motor.

KC: Ēwago mīna pogo kagaskēwatowatēyān?

You had to carry that motor and gasoline over portages too?

FC: Ēgosi mīna pogo. Mōna mīna osām wǎnaw gīnohte ispaniw.

Yes, you had to do that. He didn't want to go too far.

KC: Drums mīna gitāgonam, ten-gallon drums of gasoline.

He carried a ten-gallon drum for gasoline.

FC: Ēgatowak asici gīyayaw ēgwa asici tagoc anima piwapisk gotak gīyastēw. Ēgwa mīna anigi eight-horse Johnsons, they had a built-in gas tank. Kīspin pāwistik kāgipīcīyan kapīcipimīwēyan mōna piyātak wāna kitāpagon pāmawēsk gītwām kasopwēpaniyan māgina ōma ēgisīciwāk Kiskāciwan sīpiy. Āsay mīna gītwām inigok wānaw kayisi natayipaniyan inigok māna ēgīnītā misipōsītāsowan. Kanatayipaniyāk ōma ēgiskēnitamak ita namēwak ēyācik.

He had that and a tank for gasoline. The tank was built in on top of the motor if you ran out of

gas and had to refill the tank on the motor. The
Saskatchewan River has a very fast current. You had
to come a long way upstream with a heavy load in
the canoe. We had to drive upstream to where we
knew the sturgeon were.

KC: Tānsi māga egīsikiskenītāgik ita ēyānit
anigi namēwa?

How did they know where they are, them sturgeon?

FC: Ayō, opāpāwiyowa ētigwē ēgīwītamāgocik ēgwa
ēgīgiskanawamāgocik.

Ah, their fathers I think told them and taught them.

KC: Mōna na kēgwān gipaswātamak?

They didn't smell something?

FC: Namwāc ēgīgocipicigēcik ēgwa kēgwān
kāgacitinaman ēgota kigītasipagitawān iskok
namagwēgwān kagacitinaman.

No, they tried the fishing, and when something
was caught you set nets there until no more fish
were caught.

KC: Ayāw asici gīpagicigoskēwak?

Also, did they put hooks down?

FC: Ēgosi mina gītōtamak. Ayāwa namēpiniwi
mīcimīgwāgana kāgīyāpacitācik.

They did that too. They used sucker fish meat chunks for bait.

KC: Ēwago ana kinosēw pogo kāginaw kēgwān kigawotātāk kīspin wīmīciso.

That fish, it has to suck into its mouth if it wants to eat.

FC: Pēgwan namēpin otōn isināgwaniw māga kinwāniw anawāc wīna otōn. Ēgwa mīna ēsisak anigi nigīsinīgātānānak ēgwani mīcēt gīyapiyak owatāwa ispīk kāpagocēnāwāgok.

Yes. He has a mouth like a sucker fish. It opens wide to catch food. When you cut open a sturgeon, you could see small clams in its gut. They also took small fish like minnows. The main food for sturgeon were the small clams.

KC: Pogokēgwān na gīmīciw kinosēsa mīna?

Did he eat anything, including small fish?

FC: Ahtiht kinosēsa ēpisīsinit māga mwātēs ēsisa kāgīmowāt.

Some small fish, but mostly small clams he ate.

KC: Mōna na pogīta gīmīcisowak anigi namēwak? Ita kayāpīgamowāk ēgota na osāmpogo kāgīnatomīcisot?

Not just anyplace they would feed, them sturgeon? Where there's an eddy, is it where he mostly fed?

FC: Mōna pogīta. Ita kāpīgamowāk kātagāgiciwāk
kāminowātimik ēgwa kākinosēskānik.

*Not just anyplace. In those eddies, in the fast-flowing
current, nicely deep and where there's many fish.*

KC: Ayāw mīna asiskiy pogo ka mino nōskāk, na?

Also, too, the mud has to be nicely soft, yes?

FC: Tāpwē nahīnigok kānōskāk anima asiskiy. Ēgota
anis ēsisak anigi kāgotāwi paniwcik tahtwāw
ōma kātapasīcik. Kāgiskēnītāgik ōma māna
kāpītigēyātagānit namēwa sēmāk gāsowipaniwak.
Ēgatowāk mīna anima kāgīnatonamāk. Ita
kāpagicigoskēyāk pogo kāyāpīgamowak. Ēgwa mīna
pāmawēsk kāpagicigoskēyan pogo kigatawīnigēyan.

*True, it must be fairly soft, that mud. The small
clams would dig into the soft mud when they are run
away. As soon as they know a sturgeon has entered
their space, they dug in to hide. That's the kind of
place we looked for. Where we set hooks had to be in
the eddy. Also, before we could set hooks, we had to
clear the place out.*

KC: Māti wītamawin kāgīganawāpamat kāgotāwiyāk
kāmācītotawat mōswa. Kīna ōma kiwotācimowin.

*Tell me about the time you witnessed Dad when he
went to shoot a moose at Windy Lake where you
were trapping.*

FC: Ayō anima sīpihk isi ēgiwanīgēyāk antē Windy
Lake. Ēgīnātawē amisko wanīgēyāk anima
sipiy kāpīcistigēyāk Windy Lake. Ēgotē ēgīsi

otāpawāgok atimwak. Papiyātak anima mōna
sōgi kāgīyisicisawayāgok. Kāgīgipīcisayigēt sasci.
"Sīgac nēgi mōswak. Ōta pēyin ēgā anigi atimwak
kamigisimocik." Māga anigi atimwak ocitāw
pogo kagipīcimacik ēgwa kamigisimocik. Nīnān
nigīwāpmanānak anigi mōswak namwāc wīnawāw
anigi atimwak.

It was a river that we trapped at Windy Lake. We
had gone beaver trapping at the river, which enters
into Windy Lake. We were driving there with dogs.
We drove quietly in slow speed to there. He stopped
the dogs suddenly. "Take care, there's moose. Wait
for me here so the dogs don't bark." Surely, these dogs,
you had to silence them not to bark. Ourselves, we
saw the moose, and the dogs didn't.

Niyāganak anima kāgīgipīciyāk ispīk kāwāpamāgok
ēmatēmīcisocik ita anima kāyispācāhk. Ēgwāni
kāsopwētācimot ēnācinōstawāt. Nigīkanawāpamāw
ōma kāyitōtāk. Tātwāw ēhospikwēncik anigi
yāpēwak kāgīgipīcīt. Kāmāci mīcisonit ispīk
āsay mīna sōgi kānātātsimostawāt mitoni iskohk
gisiwahk. .22 repeating rifle ōma kāgīyāyāk. Mōna
ēgospīk nigīpimōtatānān kāmisāgi pāskisigana. .22
long-rifle bullets ōma kāgītagonamāk.

Just before we stopped is when we saw them there
on a high ridge. It was then he went crawling—he
was sneaking up on them. I was watching what he
was doing. Every time they held up their faces, those
bulls, he stopped. When they started feeding again,
then he did a quick crawl till he was close to them.
A .22 repeating rifle is what we had. Not then did
we carry the bigger guns. It was .22 long-rifle bullets
that we carried.

Ispīk mitoni gisiwāk kānātācimostawāgik ēgota
oci niga sawinawātāwak kāgītēnītāk. Ēgwa mīna
namwāc gīyocipasigō ispīk kāmācipāskiswāt.
Matwē nātawāpiyak anigi yāpēwak ēgēwāpamācik
ite oci kāpāskisōcik. Pēyak anigi yāpēwa
kāmatētatāpinatāt. Kawēsk kīwīnowak anigi
yāpēwak. Gētātawēn anima kmatē nahāpit ana
yāpēw. Ēgwāni ēnipahāt nigītēnītēn. Nāntaw
mitahāt niyānanosāp pīcipīgwāgana kāgīyāpacītāt
kanipahāt anigi mōswa.

*It is when I am so close when I crawl up to them,
it is then I can kill them, so he thought. And then
he didn't stand up when he started shooting them.
They were looking around trying to see where they
were being shot from. It was one [of] those bulls that
he kept shooting at. They were very fat, those bulls.
Suddenly, then, it sat down, that bull. It was then he
killed him, I thought. It was around fifteen shots that
he used to kill that moose.*

KC: Ēgwāni ēgīmēsciyāpacītāt inigok anima
kāsāgaskinātāt tube.

So then he actually used all that he had in the tube.

FC: Gīmēsciwēpayām anima fifteen-shot tube.
Ēgota ospigānihk kāgiyitatāpinatāt. Otēk ēgwa
oskonihk kāgīpīcistawāt. Ispīk ana mōswa kānāpit
gīmatēpōtātam mīgo. Ēgwa ēgota gisiwāk kāgīnātāt
ēntēgīsāpinatāt. Ēgwotawoci kāwāstāmawit
kapēyisicisayigēyān atimwak. Āsay kēgwāc ētitipiskāk
ōma ēgwa kiyāpic wānawīs kāyisigiwēcisayigēyāk
Suggi sakahigan isi. Ēgwāni apisīs nigīwotinēnān
wiyās. Gotaga wiyāsa nigīyaganawēnān pāgwēgin
oci. Ēgwawoti ēgota pisiskiwak kapētagopātācik

kapēmīcisocik. Mahiganak oti ēgospīk
gīmahiganskāw. Nigīyaganawēnān anima wiyās
māga vents nigīyastānān. Pīyātak kātiyāgwatīk
ēgota oci kanōskēyāw wiyās. When the meat
cools down slowly, it softens the meat. Mēsci
anima ēgosi kāgīyispanik. Gīwīgasin anima wiyās.
Nāntaw nīso pīsim māna kāgīsopwētēyāk. Mēsci
ōma ētinōtēpaniyāk mīcisowin. Ēgwāni āsay mīna
nigiyānān wiyās. Kānipātāyāk kēgwān tāpiskōc
kinosēwak pimiy gīyosītāw ēgota oci. Gīnagacītāwak
ogi kisēyiniwak.

*He used the whole tube full of fifteen bullets. It was at
the ribs that he kept shooting at. To the heart and the
lungs reached the bullets. When the moose sat down,
it was breathing out blood. He walked up to the moose
to complete the kill. He then waved at me to bring
the dogs. It was getting dark now, and we still had to
drive our dogs back to Suggi Lake. We then took a bit
of meat. The other meat we covered with the hide, so
that way the wild animals wouldn't come there to eat
it. The wolves especially; then there were many wolves.
We covered the meat with snow but had to put vents
with the cover. This was to cool down the meat slowly
to make the meat soft [like hanging meat in a cooler].
Just as he said did happen. That meat tasted so good.
We were away for two months by then. We were just
running out of meat and other food at the time. Just
then we had meat to eat. When we did hunt to kill,
like when we caught fish, he would make cooking oil.
The moose fat would also provide cooking fat. To make
the cooking oil, you had to cook the fish oil or moose
fat slowly. If you cooked it too fast, you could burn it
[rendering fat to get cooking oil by melting it]. Them
old men, they sure knew how to live off the land.*

KC: Ēgwa mīna mōswa mistahi wīnin gīyayāw.

And the moose had a lot of fat too.

FC: Ēwago anima wīnin gītīgisam. Piyātak gītīgisam.
Kīspin kiyosāmi gisisēn kipasisēn anima. Piyātak
pogo kagisisaman āskaw nipiy gītagwastān.
Kotawānāpiskohk anima katasīgaman.
Pagwānigamigohk kāginaw kāgītasīgāk. Āsay
anima ēgotē kāgīcimatēk napagamigos ēgota
kagīgapēsiyāk. Simeon Sayese, Dad, John Morin
ēgwa nīna ēgotē kāgīwāskahiganēyāk. Kinēsk
nigīyāpacītānān anima waskahiganis. Tāgōcāyihk
anta moss nigīyastānān, ēgota tāgōc poly, ēgwa
iskowānik ēgota asiskiy kāgīyastāyāk. Namwācgīyoci
ocistin. Anima roof gīminwāsin. Gīnagacītāwak
anigi kāgīyosītācik anihi wāskahigansa.
Ēgīyitāwacigēyāk anihi āpacītāwina ēgotē isi.

*That fat he would cook. He cooked it slowly. If you
cook it too much, you burned it. You have to cook it
carefully; you put in water sometimes. You cooked it
on top of the stove. He cooked it all in the tent. There
was a log cabin in place there. Simeon Sayese, Dad,
John Morin, and I had made those log cabins. We
used that cabin for a long time. On top of the roof,
we put moss, then on top of it was the poly, then the
last thing that was placed was the mud. It never once
leaked, that roof. That roof was well made. They were
very clever, the ones who built the cabins. We had
brought all the building materials to that place.*

KC: Tānspīk kāgīyitōtēwēk ēgotē?

When did you go there?

FC: October ōma kāgīyitāwacigēyāk. Nigīmisi
pōsītāsonān, lumber, sakahigana, kāginaw
kēgwān. Ēgīsi guideiwiyāk ōma āsay māna ēgota
kāgīsopwēyotēwāk.

*We took everything there in October. We filled our
canoes with lumber, nails, everything. We had
finished guiding when we would go there.*

KC: Grassberry River ōma kāgīnatayāmēk.

You went upstream on the Grassberry River.

FC: Ēgota mistahi āsay gīpāgwāw pogo
ēgīmoscipimiskāyāk, ētāgawāmāk ēgwa mīna
ēgīgāgaskwētowatēyāk āpacītāwina. Mistahi
nigīsāsīcīnān. Pogo ēgapatēnamāk ēgwa
ēgaskēwonigēyāk āsay mīna ēposītāsowāk. Mistahi
atoskēwin māga kāgīnēwogamāk namōna kinēsk
kāgīsāgamigisiyāk.

*There it was very shallow, then we only paddled, then
poled, and then we portaged everything over. We
had to take everything out of the canoe, then portage
it over, and then load it up again. Lots of work, but
then there were four of us—we worked quickly.*

KC: Ocitaw na wīnawāw ēgīwīciyēgok ēgwa aciy
wīstawāw ēgotē ēgīwanīgēcik?

*These men who came with you, were they coming
to help you, or were they going up there to
trap and fish?*

FC: Wīstawāw ēgotē ēgīwanīgēcik ēgwa mīna
ēgīnitēpagitawācik. Ocitaw kātoskēstamāsowan

ēgwāci magēgwān kigāyān kawcimīcisowan.
Namwāckēgwān welfare ēgospīk gīyociwītagan.
Gīgitimāgan ōma kayāsk.

*They were going up there to trap and fish. There was
no welfare in those days. You had to make a living
somehow. You didn't eat if you didn't go out to kill
something to eat. It was a poor time in those days.
Times were tough.*

KC: Ēgwāni anima ēgota kāgīyāyēk kigīwanīgānawāw?

*When you got to Suggi Lake, did you stay there to
continue with trapping, or what did you do there?*

FC: October 15th kāpāstenigātēk ēgwāni
kāyitatēnimāgok anigi wacaskwak osāmi pāgwānik
ita kāyācik. Nigītatenimānānak kayāgatinsicik.
Ēgwāni sōgi kāgīwaniyemāgok. Ita kātimihk
namwāc nigītasīgawānānak. Kītwām ēsīgwāk
ēgospīk ēgwani kāgīwanīgēyāk. Ēgwa asici
ēgipāpītigēcimēyāk sīpiya kanatonawāgok
amiskwak. Osām pogo nīso amiskwa kāgōtināt
pēyak wīstiy. Sāspin kamiskāk wīstiy nāntaw
nēwo gīyotinēw. Ēgwa kāpisasik wīstiy mōna
osām mīcēt gīyotinew. "Kamanācītāyan ēgāyosām
kawosāmāpanīcigēyan" gīyitwēw.

*October 15th was the open season and where we
thought the muskrats had too shallow water for
themselves. We thought that's where they would
freeze in. It was then we quickly trapped them. We
left those that were in deeper water alone. Next
spring is when we would trap them. And, too, we
paddled into rivers looking for beavers. Dad would
trap about two beavers from every lodge. At a huge*

lodge, he took four beaver. At the smaller lodges, he trapped less beaver. "You have to conserve not to overdo it, not to overkill," he said.

KC: Ēgwāni ocitaw kiwanīgēskanawāw cigēma kamanācītānāwāw. Ēgotē mōna awinak ayāw kapītigēskāgowēk.

Then for sure your trapline area you will take care of it. There is no one there to come into your trapline area.

FC: Namwāc na inigok wītigōwānaw anima kāgiyāyāk. Nāntaw sixty to seventy miles oci Cumberland. Māga ēgota ēgīpagitawāyāk mīna ocitaw ēgota kayāyāk kamiciminamāk anigi sāgahigana.

No one else wanted to come there, it was so monstrously way out there. It was about sixty to seventy miles by foot from Cumberland. Then we did fish there, and purposely we would stay there to hold on to those lakes.

KC: Nagatamēgo ēgwāni sēmāk gotak awiyāk katagopaniyo ēgota.

If you left there, so right away someone else would take over.

FC: Ēwago na kēcināc anohc ōma miciminamak kāwāgōmāyāgok Barry wānawāw. Ēgotē wanīgēwak ēgwa pagitawāyak. Pēgwāw asāy kēgāc nigīwanītānān ēgotē anima pagitawāyin. Mēsci Okanēnīcigēwak ēgīwīmīnācik anigi opagitawāyak Beaver Lake oci. Māga namwāc nigīpagitinānānak ēgosi kayitāgamigisicik.

*That is for sure, today, now they hold it, our
relatives, Barry, themselves. They trap there and fish
there too. At one time already we almost lost it there,
that fisheries. The conservation officers were going to
give it to the fishers from Beaver Lake. For sure we
didn't let them do that.*

KC: Anōhc ōma ēgwa pogīta kawotagocinak
ogwāskēpicigēwak ēgwa opagitawāyak. Ana
waskicāganīs kāyisinīgātīt kisīpaniw kinipa wānaw
kagītagocin.

*It would be easy for others to set up there since they
can go almost anywhere. That snowmobile, as it is
called, goes fast, so quickly it can travel far.*

FC: Ēgwa mīna ēsōgipicigēcik. Niyanān māgīna atimwak
kāgīyāpaciyāgok ispīk ēgotē kāpagitawāyak. Ēgwa
plane gīpēnātāstimēw kinosēwa gīgiskēmēwak
ispīk kapētagwasinit. Ispīk ētagāgāskatik sākahigan
nigīkiskinawācītānān sīcisisak oci ita katēwot plane.

*And, too, those are heavy pullers. Ourselves, no
choice then, we used dog teams when we fished there.
And then, too, an airplane came to pick up our fish.
It was arranged when to come get our fish. When the
lake froze solid, we marked out a spot on the lake
with spruce branches for the plane to land.*

KC: Ēgota ēgīpiponi pagitawāyēk ōma kāyātotaman?

Then you did winter fishing this you are saying?

FC: Ēgwāni āsay ēgīpōniwanigēyāk
kāgīmācipagitawāyak ēgospīk.

Right after the trapping, then we started to winter commercial fish.

KC: Tānitowak kinosēwak kāgīgācitināyēgok?

What fish did you set the nets for?

FC: Osām pogo atīgamēwak māga asici ogāwak ēgwa jackfishak.

Mostly for whitefish and also for pickerel and jackfish.

KC: Tāntē kāgītāwanācik ēgwani kinosēwa?

Where did they fly the fish to?

FC: Ēgota anima Beaver Lake kāgītāstimāt ēgota ēgīyastēk fish plant.

They flew them to Beaver Lake to the fish plant there.

KC: Awina kāgīpimāstimāt? Kigiskisin tānsi kāgīsinīgāsot?

Can you remember who flew them there?

FC: Parsons Airways pagāgam Creighton oci.
Ēgota gīyastēw packing plant anta Beaver Lake.
Ēgotē kāgītāstimāt niginosēmināna. Dad wīna kāgītastawācigēt kāgiskīgēmot ispīk kapētāsinit.
Niyanān māna sōgikāgīpagitawāyāk. Ēgwa mīna kātinotēpaniyāk mīciwin kāgīmīnāt masinahigan katāwēnit mīcim gītwām ispīk kāpētāsinit. Māgina misiwac magēgwān kaposītāt ispīk pētāsici kītwām.
Ēgwāni groceries gīpētāw.

*I think it was Parsons Airways from Creighton. They
took the fish to the fish plant at Beaver Lake. It was
Dad who dealt with the fish plant and when the pilot
flew our way. Us, we just fished as hard as we could.
And when we were running low on groceries, he gave
an order to the pilot to buy groceries on the flight our
way. Anyways he would fly empty on his way here.
That's how he brought the groceries to us.*

KC: Tānigok iskōk kāgīspanik pēyak ēgwācī nīso pīsim
māna ōma kāgītipōni pagitawāyēk?

How long did the winter fishing last?

FC: Nāntaw pēyak pīsim māna iskōk. Ēgwāni
kātipōniyotawācik kinosēwak ēgota
kāgīpōnipagitawāyāk.

*About one month it went to. Until there were not
that many fish being caught, then we stopped fishing.*

KC: Tānsi anigi kinosēwak ēgīginawānātagācik na Suggi
sākahiganihk?

*How were the fish, did they swim around in
Suggi Lake?*

FC: Misiwānawēstigwēyāw anima Suggi Lake.
Pāgīta ita ētimihk ēgota māna anigi kinosēwak
ēgīpītigwēyātagācik. Ēgota ēgīminowayācik.

*It is a deep, round pool, that Suggi Lake. Some places
where it is deep, those fish will swim into. Where they
have found a favourable place to live.*

KC: Ēgotē na anima Fosterihk kāyisinīgātēk?

Is that the place they called Foster's?

FC: Ēgotē nīstanān pēyagwaw nigīyānān napagigamigos. Ayāw anigi ēgīyosītācik wīstawāw napagamigosa John Morin asici Simeon Sayese. Ēgote ēgīpiponi pagitawācik wīstawāw. Marie Alma ēgwa Elise ēgota wīstawāw gīpēyāwak. Ēgīmāmawi wīcītocik wīstawāw. Isi kānipācigēcik ēgītāskītawātocik ēgosi ēgītōtāgik.

There at one time we had a cabin. It was them who made the cabins too—John Morin and Simeon Sayese. There they did winter fishing too. They came with their wives: Simeon with Elise and John with Marie Alma. They came there as a group to help each other. They helped each other and split the catch evenly among ourselves.

KC: Tāpwē ēsa kāgītagāgicik.

They did something worthy.

FC: Ēgwāni nīstanān ēgota nigīwīci pagitawāmānānak. Namwāc awinak nōtaw kāgācitināt kinosēwa nāntaw gītēnītam. Anis pēgwan inigōk kāginaw opagitawāyak gīgācitinigēwak. Ēgītaskītwātamāk kāginaw kinosēwak kāgīgācitinīcik. Ayāw mīna mīcim nigītāskītwātonān.

We, too, were there to fish with them. Nobody that caught fewer fish than the other thought much of it. It was set that all the fishers would catch the same amount. They split evenly all the fish caught among everyone. We also split the groceries evenly.

KC: Ayāw na ōma pāgwān itē kīnawāw ēgīgapēsiyēk?

So did you and Dad fish in a separate location?

FC: Namwāc nigīmāmawīnān ēgota anima kapēsiwin. Nīstanān nigīhayānān pāgwān ita napagigamos kagapēsiyāk.

No, we all stayed there at that camping spot.
We stayed at a separate place where we stayed
in a cabin.

KC: Ēgīmāmawi wīcihītowēk.

You helped each other.

FC: Ēh ēh ēgosi ēgītohtamāk. Nigīmāmawīnān ēwīcihītowak ēpagitawāyāk. Ēgwāni ispīk nōtaw ēnipahagok kinosēwak Fosterihk kāgīyācipagitawāyāk. Nētē agāmihk Suggi Lake kāgīnitēpagitawāyāk.

Yes, we did that. We helped each other to fish there.
When we started catching fewer fish at Foster's, we
moved our nets to another spot. We went across
Suggi Lake to set nets.

[In English only] We all fished together, helped each other, and split the catch with everyone. When we were done catching fish at Foster's, then we moved our nets to the other shore—the spot where the Grassberry River flows into Suggi Lake.

KC: Ita na anima sipiy Grassberry kāyisinīgātēk.

To the place where the river is called Grassberry.

FC: Mēstas ēgospīk kāgiyosītāt ēgotē
        napagigamigos wīna Dad.

        Later on, he built there a trapper's cabin
        himself, Dad.

KC: Ēgota anima kōkomisinaw Jim Carriere kāgīyosītāt
        camp. Giminwāsiniw anima cabin. Nigīgapēsin
        ēgota mēgwāc ēpipopohk.

        It is where our uncle Jim Carrîere built the camp.
        It was a good cabin. I stayed there once during
        the winter.

FC: Ēgwāni gītipōnāgamigisiw Dad ēwago pagitawāyin
        asici ēgotē kawanīgēt. Āsay anima ētiyāgosit ēgwāni
        nigīnitēskōliwin. Māga nigīmacistigwānān. Kayāsk
        aspin kāgī skōliwīyān ēgospīk.

        Then he had slowed down, Dad, that commercial
        fishing and there his trapping. Dad was already
        getting sick, and then I was going back to school. But
        then I was not learning. I had not been in school for
        a long time already.

KC: Namwāc ēgīgiskanawāmāgawiyan kayisigītāsowan,
        kayamīcigēyan, asici kamasinahigēyan.

        You didn't get taught how to count, how to read, and
        how to write.

FC: Mōna mistahi nigīskōliwin. Kītwām pogo
        ēgīgiskanawāmāgawiyān. Tagaw kāyāyān
        Kayitāniwak photographic memory. Ayāw kawēsk
        nigīhayamīcigān ēgota oci nigītigiskinawāmāson.
        Ēgwa kāgīyotinamān anigi exams tāpwē

pogo nigīmasinayēn isi kānistōtamān anigi
kagwēcīgēmowina.

*I did not go to school much. I had to be retaught. I
was lucky I have a photographic memory. And then
I read well, from there I began to teach myself. And
when I wrote those exams right away, I wrote down
what I understood for those questions.*

KC: Ēgwāni ispīk kāpōni piponipagitawāyēk Suggi
Sakahinanihk? Tānsi kigīwanīgānāwāw na sīgwani
wanīgēwin?

*When you finished winter fishing at Suggi Lake, how
then did you go trap for the spring trapping?*

FC: Aspin anima kāwatōskotēk ēgota papāsiwi
ētiwanīgeyāk asici amiskwak ētipāskisawāyāgīcik.
Ēgwa mīna atimwak kāpasocik mōswa ēgwāni
kāgospinawasēcik. Ēgwāni pogo mīna ēpēyāgok
kapētātagosīgwāw. Misiwē nigītinigānān.

*When it started melting along the lakeshore, then
we quickly would trap, and them beavers we would
shoot as we went. And then, too, the dogs would
smell a moose and then give chase into the high
ground. Then, too, we had to wait for them to come
back. A whole lot of ways we did things.*

KC: Ēgwāni ocitaw atimwak.

That is how it is with dogs.

FC: Tahtwāw kāpasocik mōswa mōna piyātak
kigīsōgānētāpāson.

Every time they smelled a moose, not carefully did you get a fast ride.

KC: Ēgwāni kāpēgīwēyēk kēgwān kāgītitasīgamēk ēgota Cumberland?

When you came back to Cumberland, what did you do there?

FC: Nigītipagitawānān ogita oci spring fishing, commercial fishing kāgītasīgamāk.

We started setting nets there for spring fishing, commercial fishing is what we did.

KC: Mōna na kigīyitōtēnāwāw spring fishing anta Suggi Lake?

You didn't do spring fishing at Suggi Lake?

FC: Mwāc ēgospīk anta Cumberland kāgīsīgwani pagitawāyāk.

No, then at Cumberland we did spring fishing.

KC: Ēgota anima Cumberland kāgīpagitawāyēk tāntowak kinosēwak kāgīgācitināyēgok?

There at Cumberland where you fished, what kind of fish did you catch there?

FC: Goldeye, pickerel, jackfish, sturgeon, egwa misagamik suckers. Ēgwāni namēpinak mistahi māna nigītātinānānak inigok ēhotawācik anapihk.

We caught goldeye, jackfish, sturgeon, and lots of suckers. Then, too, suckers. Many as usual. We took off the nets, so much they were caught in the nets.

KC: Tānsi anigi namēpinak inigok misāgamik kāgīgācitināyēgok ēgīpēyāmicik ēgwācī ocitaw ēnōtāmāmawi pimātagācik?

How is it with them suckers, so many that you caught? Were they spawning there, or do they usually swim in large groups?

FC: Ēgosi anigi kiyām egīsiyāmicik ēgwāni ocitaw māmawēntowak. Sāspin kāgācipitacik mistahi kigagēcigonigān.

That's them, never mind if they quit spawning, and then they gather in large groups. If you happen to get them, then a whole lot you take off.

KC: Ēgwa kāgīsi sīgwani pagitawāyēk Cumberland Lake kēgwān ēgota kāgītasīgamēk?

After the spring commercial fishing at Cumberland Lake, what did you do then?

FC: Nigīti namēwi pagitawānan nōmagēs. Nāntaw ēmātagimīt August ēgota ēgwa wīpicīsisak kāgīpagitawāyāgok. Ēgwa kāpōni wīpicīsi pagitawāyak ēgwāni nigīti guidiwīnan.

We started sturgeon fishing for a while. About the time starting in August, and then goldeye we fished for. And when we finished goldeye fishing, then we went guiding.

KC: Tāntē māna kāgīpagitawāyēk ēgwāni wīpicīsisak?

Where usually did you fish then for goldeye?

FC: Saskatchewan River, old Saskatchewan River ēgota gēciwak sīpihk. Old Channel anima ēgotē mīna nahinigok natimihk.

Near the Saskatchewan and Old Saskatchewan River. Old Channel, that there, not far upstream.

KC: Tānspīk mwātēs kāgīmisiyotawācik anigi wīpicīsisak?

When did you net the most, them goldeye?

FC: Kapētipisk nigīnātanapānān misāgamik nigīgācitinānānak mōna anigi misigitiwak māga mīcēt gīyotawāwak. Ēgwa nigīti pagocēnānānak. Ēgwani gēciskaw kāgīnipāsiyāk. Ēgwa kagīsi tasīgawāyāgok, nigītōtayānānak packing plant. Misāgamik pogo kagacitinācik māga gīminonāgisowak ēgwani Winnipeg goldeye.

All night long we checked our nets. We caught many. These are not big, but then many were caught in the nets. Then we gutted them out. Then we took a quick nap. When we were done dressing them, we took them to the packing plant. You have to catch many, but then they were high value—these were the Winnipeg goldeye.

KC: Kēgwān kāmīcit ana wīpicīsis? Gīmowēwak wāpagosīsa ēgwa mīna gotaga pisiskiwa atāmpēk mīna waskitipēk? Ēwago kinosēw ayāwēw wīpicsa otēnanīk. Nēhinawak gīsinīgātewak "wīpicīsis."

What did the goldeye fish eat? Did they eat mice and other creatures under water and on the water's surface? That fish has a set of very small sharp teeth on its tongue. The Cree named it "the fish with small teeth."

FC: Osâm pogo mancosa êgwa kinosêsa.

Mostly they ate flies and small fish. [In English only] No doubt they would eat other small animals they caught. They were that kind of fish. Its head and mouth looked like a piranha fish.

KC: Ana kinosêw goldeye wîpicîsis kisinîgâtânaw. Tânêgi anima êgosi owînowin? Otênanihk anima owîpicsa êgota kâstênigi.

That fish, the goldeye, we call it the toothy fish. Why call it that name? In its tongue there are small teeth placed.

FC: Tâpiskôc ana piranha kâyisinâgosit kêgâc êgosi. Kawêsk ana wîpitiw.

Like a piranha, that's the name almost like it. It does have a lot of teeth.

KC: Êgwa kâgîsi nipîni pagitawâyêk êgota kâgîmâci guidiwîyêk êgwani kîcimôkomânak otasâyigêwak asici omâciwak.

After the summer commercial fishing in August, you got ready to go guiding for the American duck hunters and moose hunters.

FC: Tāpwē ēgosi anima ēgota kēciskaw kāmisi
sōniyāgēyāk. Āskaw miscayis tips nigīmīnigoyānak
kaguidīstamāyāgok anigi. Ayāw asici inigok kāgī
tipāmāgawiyāk wīnawāw Dad kāguidiwīyāk oci.

*We would go there and guide to make quick money.
We would get tips from the hunters and always get
our pay from Dad for our guiding fee.*

KC: Moswa oci ayāpēwak na osām pogo
kāgīnipayācik omācīwak?

*Did you hunt moose for the guided hunters—like
trophy bull moose?*

FC: Yāpēwak ēgwa omānsīsak.

Bull moose and calf moose. [In English only] We
were told what to get, and that's what we hunted.

KC: Ocistāwpogo mīna ēgwaspīk gīniskiskaw ēgotē?

*It was in its nature that then there were many
geese there?*

FC: Ēgwatowak mīna gīwītāwak ēgotē. Mōna
ēgospīk gīyāpatana airboats. Tāpskōc ōma
anohc misisopweyāmōgēwak niskawa ēgwāni
oci mōna ēgota ayāwak. Niyanān māna
cīmāna ēmoscipimiskāyāk ēgwa asici engines
kāgiyāpacītāyāk. Gīminopāgwaw anima
Cumberland Lake. Ēgota oci ēgīminonōskāk asiskiy.
Mitoni gīmōnāmak ēgota maskosiya ēmīcicik. Ēgwa
mīna ēgīsīpēgoskāk.

Them, too, were there. Not then were used airboats,
just like it is now. They greatly chase away them
geese, and that's why they are not there. Us, it was
only canoes by paddling only and also with engines
we used. It was nicely shallow, Cumberland Lake.
And then from there it was nicely soft, the mud. They
would dig up there the grass to eat. And, too, there
were many weedbeds.

KC: Anigi pagacipēyāsa opimē sīpiy oci. Tānitowak
kāgīnipāyēgok nipināyisak ēgotē?

Those small inland lakes out beside the shorelines
of the main rivers. What kind did you kill, them
summer birds there?

FC: Niskak ēgwa sīsīpak. Ēgota ēgīkīwēgocīgwaw
ēgīntēnipācik ēgotē kātitipiskāk ōma. Ēgwāni
kāpētāpāk kātisāgwāstēk gītwām kāpēsopēgocīgwāw
ēgwāni ēpēnātayāgwāw sīpiya ēgwa ita
kāwānipēyīgo. Ēgotē ēpē mīcisocik kapēgīsik.

Geese and ducks. That's where they flew home to
sleep the night there. When daybreak came, again
they flew from there to come to the rivers and where
the small lakes are. There they come to feed all day.

KC: Tānsi anigi apscininsipak, pīpīcāwinisipak asici
apscisipak ēgota na gīmīcētiwak?

How about the gadwalls, widgeons, and teals—were
many of them there?

FC: Tāpwē pogītowak sīsīpak gīyāwak. Blue- and green-
winged teal ēgwāni wīpac gīwīnowak gīminosiwak.
Kātiyāgotagwāgik ēgospīk anigi maskēgosipak

kawēsk kāwīnocik. Kamistigōsīmowan namwāc
nigiwīnāwak ēgwani.

*There were all kinds of ducks: gadwalls, mallards,
teal, and others. There were muskeg ducks; some call
them fall ducks. Late in the fall, the muskeg ducks
got very fat. In English, I couldn't name them.*

KC: Ayāw anigi fall ducks or scaup isinīgātīwak.

Those ones are called fall ducks or scaup.

FC: Ēgwāni ispīk kāyosāmigāmocik, namwāc gaskītāwak
kahopawocik. Awascīna kanawāstik. Konēsk
nōcītāwak kawopipaniwcik. Kipimicisāwak
ēgwa kigītipiyāwak. Pogo kanāwstīk ēgota māna
kāgīnatonawāgok.

*Then, when they have gotten too fat, they can hardly
fly. Especially in a calm day. They will have a hard
time getting airborne. If you follow them, you can
keep up with them. It had to be a calm day when we
went to look for them.*

KC: Ēgwāni ēgosi kāgītāgamigisiwēk nocimihk
kagiyocimicisowēk?

*That's what you did when off the land, you got
your food?*

FC: Year after year, it rotated. Mōna mistahi giyoci
pōnāgamigisinān. Gotak kēgwān ēgīti tasīgamāk.
Ēgosi anima. "If you don't catch it, you don't eat. If
you catch it, you can make money. Kīspin kigītimin,
namwāc kigasōniyāgān."

186

Not much did we stop doing things. We got started on something else. That's the way it is. "If you don't catch it, you don't eat. If you catch it, you can make money. If you are lazy, you don't make money."

KC: Kātāwēyan anapiyak pogo kanānapaciyacik konēsk kagiyāpaciyāwak.

Just like the fishnets you bought, you had to take care of them to use them for a long time.

FC: Ēgwaspīk anima pāgān line, cotton line. Anohc ōgi anapiyak poly line. Ēgwa mistahi wēcipaniw ana anapiy. Kimosci agotāw. Ēgwa ēgota oci kāpāsot tāpwē pogo manipaniw anima kēgwān ēgota kāgīyāgawāpotēk. Kayās māna anapiyak nigiyagotānānak. Ēgwa ispīk kāpāsocik ēgota kāgīpēgipitāgok. Ēgwāni kītwam kātipōsipitāgok mistigwātihk āsay mīna ēgota nigīpēgipitānānak. Ēgwa ēgīginawānāt anigi anapiya kātipōsipitāt mistigwātihk. Anima oci kāyitōtāk ispīk kantēpagitawāt kawēci wanawīpitāt anigi anapiya. Gēciskaw anis pogo kapagitawāt ita sipiy kāgisīciwak. Ēwago anis Saskatchewan River ita kāgīpagitawāyāk. Mōna panta ēgosi isinīgātēw anis kisiskāciwan anima ēwago sipīy, ēsōgānēciwak ēwago sīpiy.

Back then, the nets were made of a cotton line. Today they are made of poly line. And, too, it goes very easy, that net. You just hang the nets. And, too, once dry, right away it goes off, that thing that floated onto it. And once again, while we pulled them into the box, we cleaned them too. And then Dad put them into a circular way, those nets, as he put them into the box. That there he did, for when he set the nets it would

be easy to pull out those nets. He had to set the nets
quickly where the river has a fast current. It was at
the Saskatchewan River where we set fishnets. Not
for nothing it is called the Kisiskatchewan, that there
river—it flows so fast, that river.

KC: Ēwago māna nitēnītēn, tānēgi ōgi mōniyāsak
namwāc kāgīnohtē wīnāgik kawēsk ōma sīpiy,
Kisiskāciwan ēgwāci Kisīciwan, kagīsinīgātāgik.
Wīnawāw pogo Saskatchewan kāgīyāpacītāgik.
Kayās ētigwē ēgītigocik Āpītawgosāna "Kiss my
sash, I won." Tahtwāw māna kānagatawawgocik
ēgota Kisiskāciwan sīpiy.

I wonder why the white folks couldn't call that river
Kisiskatchewan like the Métis or Indians did. They
had to use Saskatchewan. Maybe long ago they
were told by the Métis "Kiss my sash, I won," every
time they were beaten on a canoe race there on the
Kisiskāciwan River.

FC: Ētigwē [laughs]. Inigok ētigwē wīstawāw ēgi
nahipitāgwāw. Apōtigwē māgīna ēgīsāgotawawgocik
gīsōganēcimēwak ēgwāni mitoni kapēgīsik ēgosi
ēgītāgamigisicik. Ēgota oci ēgīmīcisocik kāgītimit
awiyak namwāc gīyocimīciso.

Maybe [laughs]. I think they used Saskatchewan—
for them, it sounded good. If they got mad at the
Métis, that's because the Métis were really powerful
paddlers. They were strong and didn't stop long after
a meal. If they didn't work, they were not fed. You
had to work to eat.

KC: Ēgwa mīna ēgīgistigēcik anisiniwak ita oci
kamīcisocik?

And, too, they gardened, the Indigenous people, from where they fed?

FC: Kāwāsīwiyāk māna nīstanān nigīpaskopicigānān kistigānihk. Ēgwa ispīk kīstawāw kātimisigitiyēk, kīgitāpīstamawinān kapaskospitamēk kistigān.

When we were children, we, too, had pulled weeds in the garden. And when you, too, were big, you took over from us to pull weeds in the garden.

KC: Ēgwāni māna kāgiskisiyān, pēyak nāpēw mistahi māna kāgīmiskōmīt inigok ēgīnītāwigīcigēt. Ēwago ana Joe Pelly.

And then, too, I remember one man, many times he was spoken of as a very good gardener. He was Joe Pelly.

FC: Yāh, ēwago ana mōna māgīna pogo wīna. Gīmīcētiwak anigi ēgīnītāwigīcigēcik, Fiddlerak anigi kisēyniyak. Wīsta ana Zākiyas Young gīnītāwigīcigew.

Yes, that was Joe Pelly. Was not the only one—there were many good gardeners: the Fiddlers, them old men. Him, too, that Zachius Young, was a good gardener.

KC: Wīstawāw Nābēssak.

The Nabesses too.

FC: Mīcēt anigi gīminawāsiniya ogistigāniyāwa. Ēwago anima Cumberland Delta minogin kēgwān. Kāginaw anigi gīgistigēwak kawēsk. Kāhti pōnītācik ēgwāni ēgīnagatamawācik otōskinīgīmiyāwa mostosa ōma kawopigiyācik.

There were many who had good gardens. That there, the Cumberland Delta, everything grew well. When they stopped farming, then they left it for their sons, cattle to raise.

KC: Micētāyihk isi kagīpimāciyo awiyak.

There are many ways a person can make a living.

FC: Tāpwē ēgwanima kayās mīna mostosak ēgwa mistatimak kiyāwēwak insiniwak. Kapēnīpin osām pogo nōcimihk kāgīyācik anigi pisiskiwak. Māga inigok kāgīsagimēskāk ēgotē mitoni sagisagāhk kāgīyācik. Kātagwāgik kāgīgitāmōgēyāk nōcimihk oci. Ēgosi niyanān ēgītāpacīgawiyāk. Mitoni kāgwēskas ēgota kāgīpāmipātāyāk ēwanawiyāmōgēyāk anigi mostosak asici mistatimwak.

True, that too. Long ago then cattle and horses they had, the Indigenous people. All summer, most of the time in the bush they stayed, those animals. It was because there were so many mosquitoes, it was in the thickest bushes that they stayed. When it came to fall, we then chased them out of the bushes. That's what we were used for. It was back and forth there that we ran chasing them out, cattle and horses.

KC: Kawēsk anigi mistatimwak gīyāwak mēskanāsa ēgota nōcimihk.

There was a lot, those horses had, of trails in the bush.

FC: Mitoni misāgamik gīyāwak mēskanāsa ēgotē isi
      ēgīpimicsawotocik. Ēgwa mīna gīgiskēnītamak
      ēgota oci kapēwanawiyāmocik. Ēgwāni anta
      paskwāhk ēgota kāgīgācitinayigātīcik.

      *They had so many trails where they followed one
      another. Then, too, they knew where they would come
      running out from. Once they were in the fields, they
      were caught.*

KC: Kigīmaskosīgan na kīsta? Goose Island anima māna
      itē kāmaskosīgāniwak.

      *Did you help with hay making? It was at Goose
      Island where they made hay.*

FC: Pēyak mistatim nīgiyāwāw. Ēgwani kāgīmīnak Bill
      Mckenzie "Bepboy." Kinēsk gīyotāpayēw ēgwani
      mistatimwa. Ēwago māna kāgīntēwīciwāyāk
      ēmaskosīgwēt. Ayāw māna asici nigīntēwīciyaw
      Adolphe Carriere ēmaskosīgwēt. Kīspin kinōtē
      osiyāw ten cents for the picture show on Saturday
      night. Kapēgīsik ēgi atoskēyak ten cents oci.

      *We had one horse. I gave my horse to "Bepboy," our
      uncle Bill McKenzie. He drove that horse for a long
      time. I went to help him make hay. I also went to
      help Adolphe Carriere make hay. If you wanted to
      make a dime for the picture show on Saturday night,
      you worked all day for that dime.*

KC: Kigītipāpiskonigān (weigh master) na fish-
      packing plant?

      Did you weigh fish at the fish-packing plant?

FC: Ēgota mīna nigīmasinahigēgawīn kawēsk ēgota oci nigītimaskawisīn. Anis ēgīmisiyopinigeyān 100-pound boxes of fish. Ēgwa mīna plēnīk ēgīpōsītāsoyān.

There, too, I was hired, and I got strong from there. That's when I lifted 100-pound boxes of fish. Then I had to load them into an airplane.

KC: Ēwago kāgīnohtē pētātān kayācimoyan. Anta pagitawāyin nīsta nigīntē pagitawān Suggi Sākahigan ēsīgwāk ōma. Kiyāpic anima ēmaskawāskatīk asiskiy atāmpēk. Nigiy papēcīnān kagotāyinamāk anima cīstapānātik. Māga kīna kāgīgiskēnītaman kayisitāstapiyan. Kāgēskas kāgīsiwēpiskaman cīmān mēgwāc gitītimanihk ēsitastāyan anima cīstapānātik. Mōna konēsk kāgīgotawastāyan cīstapānātigwa.

When we were spring fishing at Suggi Lake, I wanted to know one thing you did. You came there to fish with us. You knew how to get the anchor poles into the partially frozen lake bottom mud. While holding on to the anchor pole to your shoulders, you rocked the freighter canoe bow back and forth. In no time, you sank the anchor pole and got it to hold steady.

FC: Pogo kanagacītāyan.

You got to have some skills.

KC: Mona konēsk ēgota kigīyocihayān aspin kāgīsopwēyāsiyan. Matwānci kigiskisin ana iskwēw Joan Studer ēgota kāgīpimīnāt. Wīna kāgīyāwanāt kinosēwa.

Not very long there you stayed; then you flew out. I wonder if you remember that woman Joan Studer who flew there. She hauled our fish out.

FC: Yāh, nigiskisin ana wīna kāgīpimīnāt.

Yes, I remember she was the one who flew the plane.

KC: Ana mīna gotak, Berna Studer, omisa Joan kigiskisin?

There was another one, Berna Studer, Joan's sister, do you remember?

FC: Yāh, ēwago mīna gotak kāgīpimīnāt. [In English only] They were good pilots.

Yes, she, too, was another pilot.

KC: Gotak mina. Pilot, Ed LeClair.

Another too. Pilot, Ed LeClair.

FC: Ēwago mīna Carrot River ana oci nāpēw.

That one, too, Carrot River, that man came from.

KC: Ēwago ana misowē gītāgamigisiw. Tāpskōc anima kāgīpōcitēwot anima Cut Beaver River kāhociwanawīstigētīk.

That one, he did unusual things. Like this, he flew into that Cut Beaver River where it flows out.

FC: Pēgwaw anta maskēgohk gītēwo ēgwāni kāgītē tawinigēcik ēgota oci ēwanayāsit.

One time on a muskeg he landed, and then they went to clear, from there he flew out.

JOHN VICTOR CARRIERE INTERVIEW

◇

On June 10, 2020, I interviewed my brother John Victor Carriere (JVC), who still lives in Cumberland House. During his life, John has trapped, fished commercially, and guided hunters. He knows the oral and written history of the Saskatchewan River Delta, and with a critical eye for detail he continues to educate himself on the region. He is a strong advocate of blending Indigenous traditional knowledge with Western scientific ways of knowing, and he has provided valuable insights into the sturgeon fishery for studies of the species in the Saskatchewan River Delta.

KC: In this book, I mention going on a trip with Albert Flett [see the chapter "Do You Feel the Spirit of a Moose?"]. Kāgīsi opigiyāk kīnānaw Pāgwayisi Ayamiyāwin ēgitasīgamāk. Ēgwāni mēgwāc ēpimiskāyāk ita māna mōswa kāgīnipahāt. Ēgota ēgīnatonawāt. Ispīk ita kāgītatēnimāt, kāgīkagwēcimit. "Kimacsōstawāw na mōswa?"

Nigī sascimik, ēgwāni ētigwē ēgītwēt. Do you sense any sign of a moose?

The way we were raised, it was the Catholic Faith we dealt with. While we were paddling where he used to kill moose, he was looking for them there. When he expected them at that place, he asked me, "Do you feel the spirit of a moose?" He really took me by surprise with that question. He was actually asking, "Do you sense any sign of a moose?"

JVC: Yeah.

KC: In my childlike mind, the word kimacsōstawāw meant "Do you feel the presence of a ghost?" Māgīna anima ayamiwin, "macsōstawāw," it is about feeling a spirit.

I thought that saying is of a haunting. My interpretation, then, was I haunted by a moose?

JVC: The spirit is alive.

KC: In our religious experience, I began to wonder if the spirit of the moose is like that of the Holy Ghost, something mysterious, that the spirit or soul of an animal is something that could be felt.

JVC: You can interpret that way for yourself.

KC: To me now, I can tell what he was asking. Was I seeing any signs that moose were where he was expecting them?

JVC: Yes. Kitawāskayēn anigi maskosiya itē kātīsicimēyan. Kigawāpātēn ita mōswa kāgīpimātagāt. Kāti mēskocināgwan nipiy. The water will change appearance.

Yes. You part the grasses where you are paddling. You will see where the moose was wading. The water will change appearance.

KC: Kitotapoyān ita kātīsicimēyan. Kigēskināw ana apoy kītwām kātōtapowēyan. Namwāc kōpināw ana apoy pisik gitagōcimāw.

You pull the paddle as far to the side as you can where you are paddling. You turn the paddle sideways when you are going to pull the paddle again. You don't lift that paddle; it is always in the water. Canoe sneak up.

JVC: Ēgosi anima.

That's how it is.

KC: Cree and other Indigenous people believed or still believe that all animals have a spirit. It is known as animism when described by the academics. Did you ever hear of that?

JVC: No, I never did.

KC: Ocinēwin is about conservation. The act of abusing animals by killing them needlessly.

JVC: Yes, that's true.

KC: I kept snare-caught live rabbits as pets. Sometimes I couldn't bring myself to kill them.

JVC: Nigīwāpātēn na ēwago. Lettuce ēgīyasamāyēgok.

I saw that. You guys fed them lettuce.

KC: Groundhog story as told by Mom. Mēgwāskān is the meeting place [see the chapter "Where Prayers Are Called Upon"].

JVC: Anawāgēwin.

Graveyard.

KC: Macī mēgwāskān ēgota kāginaw kiga mēgwāskātonānaw.

It is a meeting place; that's where all of us will meet each other.

JVC: Ēwago anima cīpwayak owīgiyaw.

That's where the skeleton remains stay.

KC: I mentioned in the book Mom's church attendance and regular graveyard visits. We also dug up Uncle Donald McKenzie's bones.

JVC: Yes, we did that.

KC: Here's Mom's picture of her graveyard visit at Grand Rapids for the grave of her grandmother Jemima Hall, who married Bill McKenzie of Scotland. [See the photo in the chapter "Where Prayers Are Called Upon."]

JVC: Nēma kānēyāk ēgotē anima iskonigan.

That point over there is the Indian reserve.

John and I then spoke about the time that he and Franklin worked at "Little Cumberland" [see the chapter by the same name], during the construction of the "Squaw Rapids" (later E.B. Campbell) Dam, and my father and I visiting them there during the summer of 1962.

KC: Ēgospīk mēgwāc ētoskēyēk, kīna ēgwa Franklin.

That's the time you both were working there, you and Franklin.

JVC: Tāpwē ēgota kiyāpic nigīyatoskānān. That was the last job.

True, there we were still working. That was the last job.

KC: Was Joe T. Dorion Dad's friend, or was he his cousin?

JVC: That was his cousin. Kāginaw [all are] cousins, Dorions.

KC: What was his connection to Big Eddy camp?

JVC: He was running it at that time.

KC: Was Little Cumberland at the provincial recreation site across from the Thunder Rapids Lodge by the hydroelectric generating station?

JVC: Yes, it was there.

KC: Kāpēnātogiskēnimigoyēk kīna ēgwa Franklin anima ita kātoskēyēk?

He came to check, to know about you and Franklin at that place where you worked?

JVC: He probably wanted to know how much longer we would work there.

KC: Glacial till deposits from the last ice age are on this river bottom, quite visible then.

JVC: Ēgīpētāskawāt ana maskamiy. Ēgwa mīna Transport Canada ēgīpētawāpiskinigēt.

It was pushed there by ice. Then, too, Transport Canada came to push the boulders aside.

KC: Ēgwa ēgīwāsēyāgamik ēgota kāpimipaniyāk tāpiskōc gisiwāk ēpicik. Katāyipaniyacik gītēnītēn.

And it was clear water where we drove; it was as if they were sitting close. It seemed like you might hit them.

JVC: Kisēgīgok ēgīginawāpamacik. Kīna na ēpimpanīcigēyan?

You got scared when you looked at them. You then were driving?

KC: Namwāc wīna ana. No, it was him. I was only eleven years old. I couldn't see over the bow of the canoe to see where to go.

JVC: That don't matter; I was only ten years old when I started.

KC: I was too small to see where to go. He would have to point to show me where to go. No, he ran the motor.

JVC: Uncle Jim nigīpagitinik kapimipanīcigēyān, when I was ten. Aspin ēgospipaniyān sandbarihk. "Well, how about that," kāgīmoscītēt.

Uncle Jim, he let me drive the outboard motor, when I was ten years old. I drove right up onto a sandbar. "Well, how about that," was all he said.

KC: [Laughs at that famous saying of Uncle James Carriere.]

JVC: "If that was my dad, he'd be swearing like hell," I said to Uncle.

KC: Went to a junk pile by the airstrip while visiting Little Cumberland.

JVC: Ita kāgīwēpināgwāw kēgwān from the Power Station.

It was where they dumped things from the Power Station.

KC: Oskanāmōwak anigi tānsi isināgosicik?

The wasps, those ones, how do they look?

JVC: Oskanāmow is yellow and brown.

That wasp is yellow and brown, a yellow jacket.

KC: Iskwēwak [Women] who took care of my wasp
        sting, maybe the McKays.

JVC: Auntie Elise, ētigwe māga mīna.

        Auntie Elise, maybe it would be her.

KC: Most of the American hunters came from the
        northern states?

JVC: Yes, they did come from down south.[1]

KC: Picture of Bigstone River after the Tobin Lake
        Reservoir was filled. You could walk across the
        river without getting your feet wet [referring
        to a photograph at the end of the "Little
        Cumberland" chapter].

JVC: Tāpigansi gīgicistināgik ēgwaspīk?

        If only they had cleaned up the river bottom then?

*John and I then talked about the stories that I speak of in the
chapter "Waterfowl Hunting in the Early 1960s."*

KC: Stump Lake is where we went hunting.

JVC: Ēgotē [That's where] anima [it is], Stump Lake,
        pogo kagospiyan [you have to go up on] Steamboat
        Channel. It's about a mile and a half up the
        Steamboat Channel.

---

1   "Down south" is an inclusive term meaning anywhere south of "up
     north," where Cumberland House is located.

Nētē kāpētētāgwāw Stump Lake oci niskak, ēgota ēpēmōgēcik anta Steamboat Channel.

When you hear geese calling from Stump Lake, they are coming to gravel in the Steamboat Channel.

KC: Tāpwē nigīwāpamānānak āsay ēgīmatēyapicik mōgēwinihk anta Steamboat Channel. Gīyanwāstin anima ēgospīk. Māga acipogo kantēyasagēyāk anta Stump Lake. Ēgota sākahiganihk ocitaw pogo ēgota kapetipiskinsicik anigi nīpināhisak.

True, we saw them already sitting at the gravel bar at Steamboat Channel. It was calm at that time. But we were still going to hunt at Stump Lake. At that lake for sure they would overnight, those migratory birds.

JVC: Tāpwē ēgosi anima.

True, that's the way it is.

KC: Did we stay at Big Eddy camp then, or did we go back to Angling River camp?

JVC: You most likely stayed at the Big Eddy camp.

KC: Nigīpāmipimōtān ēyosawagik sīsīpak. Aspin māna ēgotē ēyitāmocik ita Dad kāmatesayigēt. Tāhto kātāyinigot gīpiniyēpayēw.

I walked around scaring out the ducks. They would go flying where Dad was waiting. Every duck that came in range he shot down.

JVC: Pāgān anis kīna pogo kapāmipimōtēyan. You did
things differently; you walked around. That was
your style.

KC: Dad's advice to goose hunters, "Shoot a goose like
you shoot a duck."

JVC: Peyagwan isi lead. Use the same lead. [Lead the
barrel in front of the flying duck.]

*And we discussed the time I went with my father and his
friends, the conservation officers, hunting geese on the
Mossy River.*

KC: The Sunday "no hunting" was in place at that time.

JVC: They should have kept it. It was changed to satisfy
the hunters down south. They wanted to hunt
all weekend.

KC: Cumberland mudflats.

JVC: Green.

KC: Cane grass.

JVC: Those are the phragmites.

KC: Caller made the right call to start shooting.

JVC: Yes, that's the way it is.

KC: The goose hunters left Mossy River camp; on their
way back home to Cumberland, they hunted ducks.

JVC: Grassy Point ētigwē kāgīyasāyigēcik. At Grassy Point, that's probably where they hunted.

We were looking at a picture of John's camp in 2006.

JVC: Kiyāpic awa mītos kācimasot. [This balsam poplar is still standing.] Ēgwa anoch [And today] this is all gone. [John was referring to an eroded shoreline in front of his cabin after many years of flooding and high-water river flow.]

KC: Back in 2013, you mentioned the Cumberland Lake shoreline was now past Frog Island. So, today, in 2020, where is it now?

JVC: What are called the twin islands is where the shoreline is now.

KC: Dad would have lived at Pine Bluff back when the Cumberland Lake shoreline was at Windy Lake?

JVC: Māga mīna [As usual], Sturgeon Fisheries asici gīwīgiyak [they also lived at] Cumberland House. Seasonal living anima ēgospīk [that was done then].

KC: Lived at Pine Bluff, then Sturgeon Fisheries, then moved to Cumberland House.

JVC: Yes, they finally moved to Cumberland for school, I think.

KC: From 2013 to 2020, how fast is the change in the Cumberland Lake shoreline by Frog Island?

JVC: It's a quick change.

KC: [Referring to a photograph.] Picture of you, guided hunter, and guide Angus McKenzie.

JVC: Angus ēgīpēgosāgētowatēt ōgi mōswa. Awa nāpēw ginosiw nāntaw ētigwē six feet, seven inches tall. Gītāwātīpēsin ōma māna kāgīpītigwēt cook shack. He was a football player.

      Angus, he carried out of the bush by himself this moose. This man here was tall, around six feet, seven inches. He would bump his head when he walked into the cook shack. He was a football player.

KC: Tāntē oci?

      Where from?

JVC: Minnesota. Angus mistahi gīyatoskēw kapēsāgētowatēt anigi mōswa. Namwāc āpo gīgaskītāwak kamicimināgik anima mōsostigwān. Ēgīyocicsāmawagik anigi. Ēgwāni nigī nagatamawāw wīna Angus kagīsipāgonāt. Ēgwāni nīna nigīnācimīcimowān Cumberland, camp oci. Ēpētagosinān, mistahi gīpōmēw inigok namwāc omācīwak ēgīwīciyīgot kasāgētowatēnit apōciga pēyak mipwām.

      Minnesota. Angus worked very hard to bring the moose out of the bush. They couldn't even hold the moose's head. I had chased the moose to the hunters. I had left Angus to finish dressing the moose. I had left to pick up groceries in Cumberland, for the camp. When I arrived, he was very disappointed since none of the hunters had helped him to even carry out one hind quarter.

John and I then reminisced about the summer of 1973, when we accompanied our father up the Grassberry River to Suggi and Windy Lakes for commercial fishing (see the chapter "On the Sacred Grassberry").

KC: I made a deal with Dad to work for him that summer. [See page 79 for the photograph showing two canoes poling up the rapids on the Grassberry River. John made the trip up the river several times.]

JVC: Kāpēgastēk ōma. Ēgota ēwīgapēsicik ēwagociy kāskwātocik.

The place of the lone rapids, that's it. This is where they will camp, why their canoes are close together.

KC: I mentioned a ritual, which you told me was passed on from the ancestors. For me, this was a transcending moment; it came out of nowhere and opened my senses to think different.

JVC: Nigiskisin anima ēgīmāgowigoyan. Māga ispīk ētisāgitayāmāk kāgīnēpīyan.

I remembered you were tensed up. Then, when we came to the lake, then you relaxed.

KC: Kamayimoscigēyan ōma ēgota.

It is where you pray, that place there.

JVC: Namwāc ēgwa ēgosi itōtamak ōgi ōta kāyācik. Tēgwac pāpītāwak ēgosi itōtamani.

They don't do that anymore, those who are here now. In turn, they laugh at it if you do that.

KC: If you want to see the Grassberry River, whose place would be good to visit?

JVC: Kagīwīcēwāw awiyak minwāsin anima kicīmān. Barry's anta Māxsihk, Derwin's anta Sākahiganihk agāmi sīpihk oci. Ēgwa itohtēni acininīsipihk Howardihk.

You can take someone with you; it is good, your canoe. Barry's place is at Max's place, Derwin's at the lake across from the Grassberry River. And if you go to Achinini River, there is Howard's. [Max's place is named after Maxwell McKay, related to our great-grandmother Marguerite McKay and kokominaw Virginie Jourdain McKenzie, daughter of Marguerite.]

KC: Grassberry River anima kanohtē itohtēyān.

I want to go to the Grassberry River.

JVC: Anta ēsa Dwaynihk pāmawēsk kasēskisiyan Pine Bluff oci ēgotē kāyāt Dwayne waskahiganis.

Then you want to go to Dwayne's before you go into the bush from Pine Bluff; there's where Dwayne has a cabin.

KC: Kisiwak Pine Bluff ita Grassberry kāmācistigētihk?

It is near to Pine Bluff where the Grassberry starts to flow?

JVC: Ēgota minwāsiniw anima cabin.

There he has a good cabin.

KC: Something about spirituality that is mentioned for mental health. Spirit users have been around for a long time. Ēgwani anigi opawāmīsak. [Those are spirit dream power people.]

JVC: Gīmāgistigēyāw, Grassberry River, anta Pine Bluff. Pine Bluff was an island. Māxsihk anta wīpac gipatin. Early total freeze-up, no travelling by canoe.

It was a wide river, the Grassberry River, at Pine Bluff. Pine Bluff was an island. At Max's place, there it freezes early. Early total freeze-up, no travelling by canoe.

KC: Anta Māxsihk iskohk Pine Bluff, "gīpagitinēwak kacīgāskopātānit otēmiyāwa"? Ēgosi na ocitaw?

There at Max's place to Pine Bluff, did they let their dogs run along the shore? Was it that way? [In his interview, my brother Franklin speaks about this and his further experiences going up the Grassberry to trap at Suggi Lake with our father.]

JVC: Namwāc na kāmigiskāk. Gīpēwak ēgota kātiyotāpāstimēcik. Ispīk Jim kāyāt camp anta Māxsihk āsay gīpōniwanīgēw Dad Suggi Lake.

Not at freeze-up. They waited there until they drove their dogs. When Jim had his camp at Max's place, Dad was already finished trapping at Suggi Lake.

KC: Ispīk ōma Franklin kāyācimāt nistam kāmāciwīcēwāt Dad kantēwanīgēnit Suggi Lake.

This is when Franklin started going with Dad to trap at Suggi Lake.

JVC: Ēgospik na Māxsihk gīgipīciwak ēgota gīyastēwa mīcet napagamigosa.

Then they stopped at Max's place. There were many log cabins there.

KC: Katisopwētēwcik ēgota oci Pine Bluff gīntēgipīcīwak. Ēgipēwocik pagāgam iskohk kawēsk kayāgwatik Grassberry River.

When they left there, they stopped at Pine Bluff. They waited until the ice was well frozen on the Grassberry River.

JVC: Tāpwē ēgosi anima ēgwa mīna ēgīntēmēskanāgēcik Pine Bluff iskōk kāpimitatinahk.

That's right, it was that way, and also they made a trail from Pine Bluff to the pine ridge.

KC: Ayāw asici kayāsowāgāw Grassberry River. Gīgociyēw Dad maskamiya kīspin ēgwanigōk gispagatiniw kayāsowāgāw.

They also had to cross the Grassberry River. Dad tested the ice to see if it was thick enough to cross.

JVC: Ēgosi na tāpwē gīnānāgacītāw ōma kātipiponik. Māga kāsīgwanik gītimānēnītam. Ēgosi māna kāgītwēt: "Mōna īgāckatwāsin sīgos." Ēgosi gīyitōtam mīna gītēwak aspin māna ēmisowēgōcīk.

That's the truth; he was watchful when winter began. But in the spring, he took chances. This is what he said: "A weasel never cracks the ice." That's what he did; then they said he fell in fully submerged.

KC: Dad's organizing of cooperative fishing.

JVC: That was the Co-op Fisheries; everyone got the equal amount of nets. Ten nets each licence holder made them equal. Cīstapānātik twenty-foot-length anchor poles for Suggi Lake fishing. You place them ten feet in the mud, five feet out of the water, and five feet in the water. Ten nets: four plus three plus three in three different locations. These were all five-inch-mesh gillnets.

KC: Tipāskāta means line up your nets in a straight line for all four or five anchor poles.

JVC: Kīspin kicācīmastān cīstapānātigwa kigīpāpiyīgawin.

If the anchor poles were crooked, you were laughed at.

MARIE LOUISE McKENZIE INTERVIEW

◇

On June 11, 2020, I interviewed one of my father's sisters, my aunt Marie Louise McKenzie (ML). She was living in Pemmican Portage at the time but has since moved just down the road to Cumberland House. She is now in her nineties. She's the aunt I spoke of earlier, the one who, like me, was flown from Cumberland House to The Pas because of appendicitis and also made the return trip home on a Bombardier snow tracker. I recorded our conversation, primarily in Swampy Cree. I transcribed the interview and then translated it into English.

KC: Ēwago kāgīnohtē kiskēnītamān ispīk kiwīcisānak anigi kāgīntēnōtinigecik agāmāskihk.

This is what I want to know—the time when your siblings, those who went to war across the ocean or to the land across the Earth.

ML: Nāntaw 1937 kāgīponipimācsit nimāmānān. Egwāni Pine Bluff nigīspicinān. Ēgotē nigīschooliwīnān

213

nīna, Elise, ēgwa Roger. Nipāpānān ēgīmīnīt ēgota
store kapimpanītwāt. Wīna ēgota Marie Alma
counterihk kāgīyatoskēt. Wīna omasinahigēw.
Tāhto sīgwan gīpētagosiniyak owanigēwak
ēpēyotinigēcik. Ēgospīk pogīta gīwanīgēwak. Mōna
anis awinak gōciyayāw trapline. Ēgwāni māna
kāpētagosincik owanīgēwak ēpēsowācik ātaya
kigameskotōnigēcik groceries oci. Mōna na nanātok
kēgwān gīyastēw anta store. Just the main things:
files, cīkahigana, ēgosi isi āpacītāwina. Marie Alma
wīna kāgīpimpanītwat anima store. Kisik mīna
ēpamīgowak. Nigī awāsiwinān ēgospīk. I was only
twelve that time. Nigī schooliwīnān ēgospik. I think
the only reason why my brothers joined the army
was that they didn't want to stay around to have
my dad keep them busy. Āsay na kipāpā Chi Pierre
gīwīgīto. Ayāw pogo Alphonse, Jim ēgwa William
namwāc na wīnawāw gīyociwīgītowak ēgospīk.
When they joined the army, my dad said he would
raise us by himself. That's what he did. He was asked
by Father Doyon if he would let us go to school at
Sturgeon Landing Residential School. John Morin
gīyitwēw āhtīt āpītawgosisānak gīpagitināwak ēgotē
kigaschooliwīcik. Tāskoc niyanān ōma orphans
nigīwīyotinigonānak ēgotē kigayischooliwīyāk.
Māga namwāc nigīpagitinigonān kāgiyopāpāyāk
ēgotē kantēschooliwīyāk. Wīna gīyopigīgonān.

It was around 1937 that our mother passed away.
Then we moved to Pine Bluff. We went to school
there—me, Elise, and Roger. My dad was given
a store to run there. Herself, Marie Alma, at the
counter she was to work. She was the record keeper.
Every spring the trappers would arrive to come buy
things. Those days they trapped everywhere. Back
then nobody had a trapline. It was then that the

trappers brought their pelts. They came there to trade for groceries. There wasn't a variety of things in the store. Main things mostly: files, axes, like those things, tools. Marie Alma herself ran that store. She also looked after us. We were children then. I was only twelve years old then. We went to school there. I think my older brothers joined the army because they didn't want to stay around to have my dad keep them busy. Your dad, Chi Pierre, was already married. It was only Alphonse, Jim, and William who were not married then. When they joined the army, my dad said he would raise us by himself. That's what he did. He was asked by Father Doyon if he would let us go to school at Sturgeon Landing Residential School. John Morin said that a few Métis were allowed to go to school there. Like us, who were orphans, they wanted to take us to go to school there. He raised us himself.

KC: Tānsi māga ēgota, kigīnawēnītēn na ōma kāgīyisipigīgawīyan?

How is it then? Were you satisfied with the way you were raised?

ML: Mistahi ninayenīten kāgīsi opigīgawiyān. Kawēsk kēgwān nigīgiskinawamāgonān kayisi pimacīsoyāk. Nistam kāgīwīgītot Veronique ēgwa ēgota oci Marie Alma. Ēgwāni nīna kāgītipamiyak kāgiyotāwiyān. He was ninety-six years old when he died. He still used to go trap even though he was already quite old. Philupsisa māna kāgīwīcēwāt kantewanīgēcik nētē isi old farm.

I am very satisfied with the way I was raised. He taught many useful things on how to make a living.

The first one to marry was Veronique, then Marie Alma, then myself, and I looked after my dad. He passed away when he was ninety-six years old. He still went trapping even though was old already. He used to go with Little Philip to go trapping by the old farm.

KC: Philupsis ana McKay ewago ana kāgīmāskisit.

Philip, that McKay, he was disabled.[1]

ML: Ēwago ana.

He was the one.

KC: Ēwago ginohtā tāpasinahigēw mīna.

He was a good visual artist too.

ML: Yah, ēwago ana. They were your neighbours. Ayāw nistam kāgiyosītāt wāskahigan Archie Goulet ēgota kāgīwīgicik.

Yes, that's him. They were your neighbours. The first house built by Archie Goulet was where they lived.

KC: Ēgwāni tāntāto awāsisa kāgīyāwācik ninīgīgwak ōma ispīk kāwīgītocik?

Then how many children did my parents have during this time of their marriage?

---

1 There were two little Philip McKays in Cumberland House. I had to make a distinction between the two Little Philips.

ML: Nistam kāgīyāwāt awāsisa kimāmā nāpēsisa. Māga, mōna konēsk gīpimātisiniwa. Ēgwāni gotaga kāgīyāwāt iskwēsisa. Bēpiscīs gīsinīgāso. Ēwago kāgīnipayigot whooping cough. Nisto awāsisa gīyāwēwak before 1940. Mōna mitoni nigiskisin ōma kāgītīspanik otē ēgīntēwīgiyāk Pine Bluff. Pāmawēs gītwām Cumberland kāgīpēyispiciyāk during the war.

The first child your mom had was a boy, but he didn't live long. Then she had a girl. Her name was Bepischees. She died of whooping cough. They had three children before 1940. I can't really remember what really happened; we were living at Pine Bluff. This was before we came back to Cumberland during the war.

KC: Gīnōtayamiw na French (Pāgwāsīmowin/ Mistigōsīmowin) isi kāgīmosōmiyān?

Did he speak French well, my late grandfather?

ML: Mōna mitoni kawēsk gīnōtāyamiw French. Māga giyamiw āskaw ocitaw pogo gīnisitōtam.

He didn't speak French that well. But he spoke it sometimes; he did understand it.

KC: Oyamiyēwigimāwa gī ayamiyēw?

A priest did he speak with?

ML: Mācigostān ōma otācimowin. Namewa ēntēsamāt oyamiyewigimāwa Father Waddēl gītāw. Omisi kāgītigot French eyaminit, "Ēgwa mīna awa ēpēsamit nāntaw ēgwa mīna kēgwān

217

ēpēnatotamawit." Ēgwāni ēsa kāgītāt, "*Mon Pere
mōna na kegwān ēntēnītamātān ōma kāpēsamitān
namew. Ēpē moscih asamitān ōma.*" Ēgosi kāgītāt.
[Laughs at the idea that he had understood what
the priest had said about him in French. The priest
thought that he wouldn't understand him at all.]

*I will give an example; this is his story. A sturgeon
he went to feed the priest; Father Waddel he was
called. This is what he said to him in French, "Once
again he comes to give me food; there is something
he wants to ask from me." This is what he said to him
then, "Father, I don't want anything from you for
this sturgeon. I only came to give it to you as a gift."
This is what he said to him in French. [Laughs at
the idea that he had understood what the priest had
said about him in French. The priest thought that he
wouldn't understand him at all.]*

KC: Gīgaskītāw ocitaw pogo kapāgwayisīmot [French].

He was able to speak French.

ML: Ayāw ana mistahi gīyamiw French, Solomon,
Leonile's older brother. Ēgīwīcitēmāmāt
Oyamēwigimāwa ēgota oci kawēsk gīyamiw French.

*The one who spoke a lot of French was Solomon,
Leonile's older brother. He used to play cards with
the priest. From there, he spoke French well.*

KC: Nimosom ēsani na, French, Cree, and English
gīgaskītāw kayamit.

*My grandfather, then, he was able to speak French,
Cree, and English.*

ML: Mōna mistahi gīyapacītāw English ēgwa apisīs pogo French. Osāmi pogo gīnēhinawēw. Māga ispīk kāgīschooliwīyāk pogo English kāyamiyāk.

Not much did he use English and a bit only of French. Mostly, he spoke Cree. But when we went to school, only English we spoke.

KC: Ayō anigi tāhto kāgīyopigīyacik kōsisimak kāginaw gaskītīwak kanēhinawēcik?

For those you raised, of your grandchildren, can all of them speak Cree?

ML: Mīcēcīs ōgi nigīyopigiyāwak. Māhti: Derwin, Dwayne, Robin, Veronica, ēgwa Jacquie ēwago kawēsk gaskītāw. La Ronge ayāw ēgotē ēnursīwit. Ayāw awa ōta mēgwāc kāwpigiyak Glen's son. Nisitōtam apisīs māga mōna ayamiw. Kāgitotak ōma ēgota ninatōtāk ātawina. [Laughs about that.]

I raised many of them. Let's see: Derwin, Dwayne, Robin, Veronica, and Jacqueline, who can really speak Cree. She lives in La Ronge, works as a nurse there. The only one who is here now I am raising is Glen's son. He understands a little bit; he doesn't speak it. When I scold him in Cree, he listens to me at least. [Laughs about that.]

KC: Pogo kagitotat ōma kasasīpīcasit.

You need to scold when he doesn't want to listen.

ML: Ēgosīna.

It has to be that way.

KC: Tānispik Cumberland kāgīpēspiciyēk?

When did you move to Cumberland?

ML: Ispik ēti pōni nōtintonāniwāk. Ēgwāni gītipētātagosiniyak kāgīntēnōtinigēcik. Ayāw nistam ēpētagosik kipāpā ēgīmisōt namwāc aniwāk gīnōtinigēw gīpagitināw kapēgīwēt.

Just when the war was ending—that time they started coming home, those who went to war. The one who came home first was your dad. He had been wounded and couldn't fight anymore. He was allowed to come home.

KC: Tānsi kigītēnimāwāw ispīk kāpētagosik? Kigīgoskwāpsināwāw na?

What did you think of him when he came home? Were you surprised at the way he looked?

ML: Nigīgiskēnītēnān egīmisot. We were kind of expecting that he was to look different after he got wounded. Mōna nigīsastāpisinān. Tāpskōc Alphonse, as a prisoner of war. Ēwago mīna gīgiskēnītāgosiw. It would affect them somehow. We remembered your dad: ēgīgīginawānopātāt mēgwāc ētipiskāk tāpiskōc ēsayigēt wīsta Elise gīgiskisiw. Tāpiskōc kāyitōtāgik māna kāntēnōtinigēcik.

We knew that he was wounded. We were kind of expecting that he was to look different after he got wounded. We did not see it suddenly. Like Alphonse, as a prisoner of war. Him, too, we knew the way he was. It would affect them somehow. We remembered your dad: he would go running around during

the night like he was looking for someone. Elise
remembers that too. Just like they would do when
they went to fight.

KC: Māna tāpiskōc ēgīgīskēpanit?

Was it like he had lost his mind?

ML: Mōna na mitoni māga ēgosi gītēwak tāpiskōc
ēgīgīskēpanit. Gētātawēn māna ōma kaminīgēcik
ēgota māna sasci kāgīnōtintocik.

Not completely, but they said it was like he lost his
mind. All of a sudden, while they were drinking,
that's when they would fight each other.

KC: Ēgwa ispīk ita nitāwi kāgīwīgicik tānsi māna
kāgītātsit?

When my dad would go home, how did he behave?

ML: He was all right there. Gīntēwanīgēw wīsta
ōtē kātātskāk nantaw 1946. Gīwanīgēw kawēsk
ēgotē. Māga ispīk kāmāci minīgēcik ēgota māna
gīyatimāmitonēnītamak. Ēgwāni ōma kāminīgēcik
anta downstairs nīgiwāk kāgīmahtēyācimocik
ōma kāgītagamigisicik nōtintonānihk. Āskaw
nigīpētawānānak ēmatē acimocik upstairs oci ita
kāgīyāyāk. Kāgīmatēyācimocik ōma kāgīsipamīcik.

He was all right there. He went trapping, too, at
Bloodsucker Lake around 1946. He trapped really
well there. But when they started drinking, that's
when the memories of war came. When they were
drinking downstairs in our house, that's when they
told stories of what they did in the war. Sometimes

*we heard them telling those stories from upstairs
where we stayed. They would tell stories of how they
were treated.*

KC: Alphonse āsay wīsta ēgota gīyāw? Ēwago mistahi
gīgwātagiyāw.

*Alphonse, he, too, was already there? He was greatly
mistreated.*

ML: Āsay wīsta gītagosin. Ēh ēh mistahi gīgwātagiyāw.
Ēgwāni māna kāgīyātotāk mīcētwāw ēgīnōtēgatēt.
Ēgwani kāgīmīcit maskosiya. As far as he could
reach, ēgīyoci otināk kigamīcisot. Pēyagwan
tāpiskōc mostos.

*Already he came back. Yes, he was greatly
mistreated. There again he would tell of the many
times he was hungry. Then he began to eat grass. As
far as he could reach, he would take it to eat. Just
like a cow.*

KC: Ispīk kāgītagosīk tānsi kāgīsināgosit?

When he came back, how did he look?

ML: When he arrived, he was ninety pounds in weight.
Mistahi gīpāwanīw inigok ēgīwanītāt weight.
Māga he was clean. Pāmawēsk kēgwān kigamīcit
pitamā pogo kapasot. Pogo kēgwān gīnānāgacītāw
kigapēgwanik. Tāpiskōc kapēgīcigēyāk
gīginawāpātam kīspin kāmamānīsiyāk. Ēgwa māna
kawēpawayigēyāk kīspin kāmamānīsiyāk "Kītwām
wēpawayigēk," kāgītigowāk.

When he arrived, he was ninety pounds in weight. He was very skinny, that's how much he lost in weight. But he was clean. Before he would eat something, he would smell it first. Everything that was there he watched carefully to see if it was clean. Just like when we cleaned up; he would look over to see if we missed a spot. "Sweep again," he would tell us.

KC: Gīgiskēnītam ēsa anima pogo kapēgiyot awiyak ēgwāci ōma kagīyāgosin ēgota oci. Tāpiskōc ōma mēgwāc kāyitāgamigāk, COVID-19. Namwāc kāgīmaciyowisin. Kawesk kagiyāgosin egota oci.

He knew then that you must be a clean person, or you might get sick from not being clean. Like it is now, what is happening with COVID-19. You can't be a bit unclean. You can get really sick from that.

ML: Yeah. We are lucky right now nobody has it here.

KC: Māga pāgān itē oci awiyak kagītagōtatāw. Ēgosi nōtāyispaniw.

But now from another place someone can bring it in. That usually happens.

ML: Yāh!

Yes!

KC: Pēyak kēgwān kāgiyogāwiyān nigītigonān, "Awiyak wītāw ēnānāgacīgoyāk. Kiganawāpātēstamāgawinaw ōma kīnānaw Anisiniwak."

One thing my late mother had told us, "Someone exists who is looking out for us. We are being looked upon, that is we the People."

ML: Ēgosi māna, wīstawāw nigītāwak ōgi niwīcāmāganak, "Kiginawāpamigōsinānaw, ōma kīnānaw."

That it is, they, too, I have told them who live with me, "Some unknown entity is carefully watching over us."

KC: Kīsta mīna ēsa kinisitōtēn ēwago.

You, too, then understand that.

ML: Kinawāpimigosiwak ocitaw pogo wīstawāw ōgi ansiniwak. Mōna pogo kasgitēwīyāsak wīstawa mistigōsiwak. Mīcēt egota nōgosiwak mistigōsiwak. Ēwīcimarchīmācik anigi kasgitēwīyasak. Ēwago mīna anima oci mīcēt anisiniw gitimahiso minīgēwin kāyāpacītāt asici maci maskīgiya kāwotināk. Ocitaw pogo, anisiniwak kanāgatēnimisocik.

They are being carefully watched for sure, them other humans. Not just the Black people, them, too, the white people. Many are shown there, the white people. They are marching with the Black people. There is another thing—many a person hurts themselves when using alcoholic drinks and taking bad medicine. They must, all humans, take care of themselves.

KC: Kāgīwīgiyēk ita kīnawāw kāgopigiyāwasoyēk ēwago nigiskisin?

Where you lived yourselves, when you raised children that I remember?

ML: Nētē opime kāgīyāyāk niyanān. Āpītawigamigok ēgota kāgīpiminawāsoyāk. Gotawānāpisk ēgota gīyapiw. Wīna gotagīk kimosōm gīpeyago ayāw.

Over there elsewhere, that's where we were, us. In the middle part of the home is where we cooked meals. A cooking stove was sitting there. He at another place your grandfather stayed alone.

KC: Ēgota anima, kāgīyāt ēwāsīwiyān nigiskisin. Ēgīpēwīcigapēsīmāyāk niyanān nāpēsisak kāyisiwāgōtowāk.

Where it is he stayed as a child, I remembered. We would come to camp with him, we boys who were all related.

ML: Ēh ēh ēgosi anima.

Yes, it was that way.

KC: Nigīyasogwāminān nisto nāntaw pēyak nipēwin. Ispīk kāgisēpāyāk, porridge gisēpāmīcisowin kāgīpiminawātigoyāk pāmawēsk kātigīwēyāk. Ēgwa mīna nigīwīcipōsīmānān kantēnātanapēt. Ēgota anima cīki sākahigan Cumberland Lake kātipītigēciwak Bigstone River. Ēgimoscipimiskāt cīmānis.

We slept together about three of us in one bed. When morning came, porridge as a breakfast he cooked for us before we went home. Then, too, we went for a ride with him when he went to check a fishnet. It was there beside the lakeshore of Cumberland Lake, just where it flows into the Bigstone River. He just paddled a small canoe.

ML: Ēh ēh.

       Yes.

ELISE SAYESE INTERVIEW

◇

his interview took place on March 16, 2020, in my
aunt Elise Sayese's (ES) home at Young's Point south
of The Pas. She was the youngest child born to my
paternal grandparents, Leonile Carriere and Agnes
Morin. Below she speaks of the suffering her brothers experienced after they returned from serving with the Canadian
Armed Forces during the Second World War in Europe. She
recalls the things her brothers told me, and I am more than
grateful for her honest comments and memories. More pos-
itively, my aunt and I also discussed family history and some
of her recollections of growing up. Most of our conversation was in our Swampy Cree, which I have done my best
to translate into English; sometimes, though, we used both
languages interchangeably.

KC: Tānspīk nitāwipan kāgītagosīk agāmaskihk oci ispīk
      kāgīmiswāganīgātīt?

      *When did my late father return from across the other
      side of the Earth when he got wounded?*

ES: Wīna nistam kāgīpētagosik inigok owīcisāna kāgīntēnōtinigēcik.

He was the first one to return home from all the siblings who went to war.

Aunt Elise recalled my father's words.

"Nigīwitamāgonān micētawāyik nigīpēpōsin ōma ita kāpētagosinān."

He told us, "I have been in many vehicles to get here where I have arrived."

"Ana nāpēw kāgīmiskawit ispīk kāgīmiswāganīgātigawiyān nigīpimwatāmik iskok ita kapōsīgawiyān. Tāpiskok cart ana ita kāgīpōsīgawiyān."

"The man who found me when I got wounded carried me to the place where I got taken in. It was like a cart where I got a ride in."

Ita kāgīpōsiyācik simāgansīgana kāgīmisomīt. Ēgwāni ētigwe Red Cross ita kāyācik kāgītōtayīt. Mōna mistayi kegwān giyocigiskēnītam ōma kāgīspanīgot. Ispik ita kāgītiminowayāt kāgīpēgīwēcisawot.

Where he was put into was where the wounded soldiers were put. Then I think the Red Cross is where they took him. He wasn't aware at all what had happened to him. When he got better is when they sent him home.

KC: Ana kāgīpimwatāmāt ēwago "Whitey"
kāgiyisinīgātācik. Frank Chaboyer ana owīnowin.
Kāgīsipētaman ācimowin anima kāgītāpinatīt
kagīnipit ēgota oci mistawi ēgīmīgowit. Mēsci āsay
ēgīpīciyēpinācik mīwayi maskimotihk. Ēgota anis
kāpīciyēpinācik ana kānipit awiyak.

The one who carried him was "Whitey," as he was
called. Frank Chaboyer is his name. The way I heard
the story, the way he was wounded, he should have
died he bled so much. They were about to throw him
into a body bag. This is where they throw someone
who is a dead person.

ES: Ēgota ana Whitey kāgītāt anigi, "Kiyāpic awa
pimātisiw." Ēgwāni kāgīsopwētatāmāt ita
kantēnatawiyīt.

That's when Whitey told them, "He is still alive." Then
he carried him away to where he could get treated.

Ēgota gotak nāpēw gīpimiwatāmēw wīsta.
Nīpawawinihk oci. Inigok kāgīmiswāganīgātīt
gīgēcināwak āsay ōma ēnagatasket. Māga kiyāpic
gisopwē pimwatāmēwak hopitalihk iskôk.

There was another man who carried him too. He
was from Nipawin. They thought because of the
extent of his wound that he was dead. However, they
still carried him into the hospital. [My brother Les's
recollection: "The soldier's name from Nipawin was
Edward Fast."]

Nipawin ana oci nāpēw nigīyācimostāk. Wīna
ispīk ēgītōtēt Regina. Ēgīwīsāmīt kigantēyamit.
Ispīk emiskômīt wīna ōma ēgwa kantēyamit.

"Kāsāgēpātāt ana ēwago nāpēw Nīpawawinihk
ōci ēpēwāciyēmit." "I didn't think you would be
alive!" kayisit.

*The man who came from Nipawin, he [your father]
told me about him. He [your father] had gone to
Regina. He had been invited to speak there. When
it was announced he was to come up to speak, "He
came running out, that man from Nipawin, to come
shake my hand. 'I didn't think you would be alive!'"
he said to me.*

KC: Māgīna mistahi ēgītāpinatīt.

     It must have been how badly he was wounded.

ES: Mitoni owīgwāgan inigok ēgīpīgatahigātēnik.
Kēcināc gītēnītamak namwāc kagīpimātisit.

     *His face was so badly broken up. They thought for
sure he should not be alive.*

KC: Kātagosīk anta ispīk kāpōninōtinigēt, tānsi
kāgīpēyisipimōtēwot?

     *When he arrived after he stopped fighting, how did
he travel?*

ES: Ēgwāni Halifax nistam kāgīpētagosīk. Ēgwāni
ēgota ohci kāgīsopwēpimōtēwot. Omisi kāgītēt,
"Nanātōk otāpānāskwak nigīpēyācipōsin. Ēgwa
nistam kāpētagosinān misticīmān nigīpēpōsin."
Gītwēw, "Ēgwāni ēgota ohci trainihk nigīpēposin
iskōk ōta Opāskwēyāhk. Ēgota kāgīpēyit nistēs
Jonas miscacimosisa pēyak ēgīwotapayāt. Ēgota
kapēgīwētāpāsit iskohk Cumberland."

*It was in Halifax where he arrived first. Then from
there he started travelling. This is what he said, "I got
to ride in all sorts of vehicles. When I first arrived
there, I came in a big canoe [ship]." This is what he
said, "From there, I took a train ride right up to The
Pas. It was there that my brother Jonas waited for
me. He had driven a small horse there. This is how I
came to Cumberland."*

KC: Cumberland kāpētagosīk tānsi ēgota kāgīsināgosit?

When he arrived in Cumberland, how did he look?

ES: Mīcētwāw gīpētagwāmo my sister-in-law,
Sōminis. Mistahi ētigwē ēgīmīnīt maskīgīya
anima kāgītāpinatīt. Nōtaw aniwāk kagwātagītāt.
Kāgīpaspāpiyān māna wāsēnamāwin. Ēgota
kāgīwāpamak ēpāmigīnawānopātāt wāskahiganihk.
Tāpiskōc awiniya ēyasawāt. Tāpiskoc pāskisigan
ēmicimināk.

*Many times she came running to us, my sister-in-
law, Sōminis [my mother's nickname]. I think he had
been given many types of medicine for his wounds.
It was to lower his suffering. I would look out the
window. That's when I saw him running around the
house. Just like he was watching someone. Just like he
was holding a gun.*

KC: Ēwago anima PTSD, kāyisinīgātēk.

That is PTSD, that's what they call it.

ES: Ēwago anima kēcināc ēgīyāt. He must have had to
take powerful medicine to kill his pain.

Those things affected him. Those would have to wear off too.

It is for sure what he had [meaning PTSD].

KC: Māskōc gīwīsagāpinēw tāpitaw.

He must have been in great pain all the time.

ES: Ēgospīk nigīwīcāmānān kāgīyopāpāyān: Nīna, Marie Louise, ēgwa Roger. Āsay wīnawāw Veronique, ēgwa Marie Alma pāgān itē ēgīwīgicik. Ēgwāni māna kāgīpēgiyogēcik anigi kāgīntēnōtinigēcik kāgīpēminācik opāpāyowa. Ēgwāni māna kāgīsopwēnōtinocik.

It was then we still lived with our late father: me, Marie Louise, and Roger. Already Veronique and Marie Alma were living elsewhere. It was then they would come to visit, those who went to war. They came to give their father a drink. It was then they would start fighting each other.

KC: Tāpwē kāgīyogāwiyān māna nigīwītamāgonān kāgītātisicik ispīk kātigīskēpēcik, "Pēyagwan atimak ēgīsi notintocik kātigīskwēpēcik."

That's true, my late mother told us how they behaved when they got drunk, "Just like dogs they would fight when they got drunk."

ES: Ēh ēh ēgosi gīsāyāwak. Mistahi gītimayitowak kāgīsinōtintocik. Ēgwāni ēgosi kāgīsipētātagosincik nistēsak pāpāgān ispik. Ēgwāni nistēs Jim pīnisk wīsta gīpēgīwēw. Kimāmāwihk kāgīpēgipīcīt. Nigītik nipāpā kantēwāpamak ēgtotē. Māga ēgospīk

nigiyagisken miskotāgway ēgīyatāmāgok Sisterak.
Kīginowgan anima miskotāgway gimānācasin.
Fur trim gīyastēw ēgwa kīgīsowayāw. Montreal
gīyohci paniw. Ēwago nipapa kāgīyatāwēstamawit.
Ispīk Jim ēwāpātāk niskotāgway, omisi kāgīyisit,
"Nisīmis tāpwē mānātan ōma kiskotāgway. Tānsi
awa kipāpānaw ēgīsi apaciyāt sōniyawa māna
kāgīpēsicisāmawak. Sēmāk kigawītamawāw
gotak miskotāgway kanātsāmāsk. Sōniyāwa
niga mīnāw kīna oci." Ēgwāni kāgīpētagopanik
gotak miskotāgway ēminwāsik asici astotin. A
matching hat.

*Yes, they behaved that way. They were not kind to
each other the way they fought each other. That was
the way they arrived, my brothers, at different times.
Then my brother Jim finally came home. He stopped
at your mom's house. My father told me to go see him
there. Then I wore my coat, which we bought from
the Sisters. It was a long coat and was a bit worn
looking. It had a fur trim and was warm to wear. It
came from Montreal. This was what my dad bought
for me. When Jim saw the coat, this is what he said,
"My little sister, it is really bad looking, your coat.
What did our dad do with the money I usually sent
him? Right away you tell him another coat to send
for you. I will give him money for you." It was then
that it came here, another coat, very nice with a hat.
A matching hat.*

*We then went on to speak about our family's history on my
father's side.*

ES: My father remembered that they had a place
        near Saint Boniface Hospital [near the forks of
        the Assiniboine and Red Rivers in what today

is Winnipeg] before they had to flee from there [following the 1869–70 Red River Resistance].

KC: Ana Jonas tāntē kāgīyocīt wīna? Kipāpā anigi second wife ēgwācī nistam kāgīwīgimāt anigi iskwēwa?

What about Jonas, where did he originate from? Was it from the second wife or from the first wife he [my paternal grandfather, Leonile] married? [Jonas was my father's older brother.]

ES: Jonas ana wīna kāgīwīgimāt Suzanne Michel.

Jonas was the one who married Suzanne Michel.

KC: Ayō anima kāgēcimitān awinta kāgīyocīt awa Jonas. Nistam family kayāwāt Leonile ēgwācī gotagik oci?

What I wanted to know is which family Jonas came from, was it the first family Leonile had or another?

ES: Nistam nisto giyāwēwak, Isidore, Jonas, ēgwa Rosalie. The second wife had only one child, Catherine gīsinīgāso. I know she [Catherine] became Charlie Head's wife. Ēgwani ana Nipāpā his second wife, Felix Fosseneuve owicisana. Charlie Head and Catherine gīhayāwēyak Louisa Cook, Sarah-Cicimā, ēgwa Albert Head.

The first family had three children, Isidore, Jonas, and Rosalie. The second wife had only one child, Catherine was her name. I know she [Catherine] became Charlie Head's wife. [Leonile's] second wife was Felix Fosseneuve's sister. Charlie Head and Catherine had three children: Louisa Cook, Sarah-Cicimā, and Albert Head.

KC: We are related to many.

ES: From that, there are many we are related to. Us, then, from his third wife. Agnes Morin was her name, that's where we came from.

KC: Ēwago ana Agnes Morin kigīgiskēnimāwak na your grandparents?

Her, then, Agnes Morin, did you know your grandparents?

ES: Namwāc nigīgiskēnimāwak. Ēgwani ana pogo Nōcigē Āshēlik kāgītīt.

I didn't know them. It was only Nochigay Angelique [my paternal great-grandmother], that's what they called her.

KC: Nōcigē Āshēlik Dorion ēgotē oci anima maskasowin kāyocipanik. Ana māna nimis Anne wīna tāpwētam ācimowin tāpiskōc ēgotē kōyocīcik anigi Dorionak anima Missouri Country kāyisinīgātēk. Ēgwaspīk pēyak Iskwēw gīwīcēwēw anigi kīcimōkomānak nistam West Coast kāgītōtēwocik. Ēwago iskwēw kāgīwīgimāt anigi nāpēwa ēgīmasinawagēwīt kagiskinōtawāt Lewis and Clark Expedition. Onāpēma ana iskwēw gīnipayimāwān itē ēgīmisinōtinigēcik. Ēgota oci gisopwēyāmo ana iskwēw. Wīgātaw gīwīgimēw Doriona ēgota kāyocīt ana Angelique Dorion. Solomon ēgwa Leonile ēgwani ogāwiyāwa. Ēgota oci Pwātak gigāciwāgōmānānak. Ēgwa mīna Apītawgosisānak kiwāgōmānānak.

*This Nochigay Angelique Dorion, that's where the
strength comes from. It is again my sister Anne's
belief, the story where the Dorions came from. It is
from a place they called Missouri Country. There
was a woman who travelled with the longknives
to go to the West Coast. The woman who travelled
with them was married to a guide for the Lewis and
Clark Expedition. Along the way, the man was killed
in a battle. That was when that woman fled from
there back to her community. Later she married a
man named Dorion—that's where Angelique Dorion
comes from. She was Solomon and Leonile's mother.
We are somehow related to the Dakota Indians and
the Métis. [Solomon was my paternal grandfather
Leonile's brother.]*

ES: Ēgosi ana nigītigonān kāgiyopāpāyān, "Nigīwīginān
       mēgwāc ita kācimatek, Saint Boniface Hospital.
       Mēgwāc ēgota wāskahigan ēgīyāyāk. Ēgota
       oci kāgīpēsopwēyāmowāk." Ēgota oci Nōcigē
       Āshēlik kāgīpēsowāt nīso oskinīgīsa. "Mīcētwāw
       nigīpēgipīcīnān," gītēw, "cīmānihk ēpōsiyāk." St.
       Laurent mīna gīgipīcīwak. Ēgwāni pīnisk Grand
       Rapids kāgīgipīcīcik. "Āsay nigīmisigicsin," gītēw.

*This is what was told to us by our father [Leonile],
"We lived where it stands, Saint Boniface Hospital.
This was when we had a house there. This was where
we fled from." That's where Nochigay Angelique
brought the two boys. "We stopped many times," he
said, "riding in a canoe." They stopped at St. Laurent
[the historic Métis community on the southeast shore
of Lake Manitoba]. Then finally at Grand Rapids [in
Manitoba, between Cedar Lake and Lake Winnipeg]
they stayed. "I was already a bit big," he said.*

Grand Rapids ēgotē kīgīsīgātāwīt. Ēwako oci
tāpiskōc ēgota kāgīnītāwigit. Saint Boniface
ana kāgīyocihopigit. Mīcētwāw nimītātēn ēgwa
ēgīmasināmān ēgwani acimowina. Ēgwa āsay
ēgīnītāwi masinawigēyān.

*Grand Rapids was where he was baptized. It was as
though there was where he was born. Saint Boniface
was where he was raised. Many times I regret that I
didn't write those stories. Already I had been able to
write well.*

KC: Tāntē kigīgiskinawamāgawin?

Where were you taught?

ES: Pine Bluff ita kāgīwīgiyāk.

Pine Bluff, where we lived.

KC: Awina kāgīgiskinawamāgēt?

Who did the teaching?

ES: Sicotte.

Sicotte.

KC: Ēgwāni ēgospīk ana Jonas kāgīpētagotāpātāt
nitāwiya miscacimosa oci.

*That time when Jonas came riding in with my dad
using a small horse.*

ES: Miscacimosa asici otāpānāskos gīpētagopaniyak.
Barrier Lake ēgota gīpēgipīciyak.

A small horse with a small sleigh they came riding in. Barrier Lake is where they stopped. [Barrier Lake is halfway between The Pas and Cumberland House, on the Saskatchewan-Manitoba border.]

KC: Alphonse, māga tānspīk kāgīpētagosik?

Alphonse, when did he come back?

ES: Ēgīyotinīt anima ita kāgīnōtinigēt. Wīna iskowānik kāgīpētagosīk. Āsay ēgīpōni nōtintonāniwak. Ispīk kātagosīk mistahi gīpāwanīw.

He was taken prisoner where he was fighting. He was the last one to come back. The war was over by then. When he arrived, he was very thin.

KC: Ēgīgitimāgāgatisot.

He was terribly starved.

ES: Mistahi gīgitimāgāgatso. Ēgwāni mīna ēgota oci gīminīgēskiw. Ayāw anima kāgīsāyāt Simāgansīgānak Otāspinēwiniyaw, PTSD itamak.

He was so terribly starved. From there on, that made him drink too much alcohol. What I think he had was the soldier's sickness, PTSD they call it.

KC: Ēgwāni ētigwē inigok ēgītāpinatīcik. Anis mōna gimanāciyāwak anigi kāgīyotinīcik Simāgansīgānak.

Surely that's how badly wounded they were. They were not spared, the prisoners of war.

ES: Ēgwāni kāgīyācimāt Makōsa Victor Nabess wīsta
ēgīyotinīt. Gītagāgācimēw, "Mōna ōta niwiyayān"
kāgītigot. "Ēgwāni aspin ēsopēpātāt misowēta
mōsiniya ēpāgītinigi. Ēgwāni ētoge kanipayīt
nigītēnimaw."

*It was then he [Alphonse] told the story of Makoos
Victor Nabess; he was a prisoner too. He [Alphonse]
told an incredible story about him. "I don't want to
stay here," he [Victor] told him. "It was then he ran
away," [Alphonse continued]. "All over the bullets
were falling. I thought for sure he would get killed."
["Makoos" was Victor's nickname, origin unknown.]*

KC: Māga gīpaspīw.

But then he made it.

ES: Macāyīs ana Makōs ēgwāni ēgīpaspīt. Kīgaskītāw
kagicskīt. Alponse kāgītēt, "Ispīk gītwām
ēwāpamak, nigītāpētēn ēgīgaskiyot. Mitoni anis
nigīgēcināwon kiganipayīt."

*The devil that Makoos, he made it. He was able to
get away. Alphonse said, "When I saw him again, I
believed then that he got away. I was certain he was
going to be killed."*

KC: Māga gigaskiyo.

But then he got away.

ES: Tānsi ētigwē kāgītōtāk? Āpōtigwē gīnipōgāso
ēgwacī gīnītāgāso.

How did he do it? Maybe he played dead, or he knew how to hide.

KC: Nigīwītamāk kāgīyogāwiyān, "Ēgīmīnīcik anigi Simāgansīgānak awasimē kantē giskinomāsocik ēgotē oci atoskēwina kagācitināgik. Māga wīnawāw ōgi Cumberland veterans namwāc pēyak gīyociwotinamak ēwago asotamākēwin. Tānēgi ētigwē kāgīyotōtāgik ēwako anima?"

She told us, my late mother, "They were given, the soldiers, an educational advancement from which they could get jobs. But then the Cumberland Indigenous veterans, not one of them took up that promise. Why did they do that?"

ES: Anawāc ētigwē anima kāgītōtāgik kayātē kāgīsipimācīsocik. They would rather fish and trap like before they went to war. Ēwago ēgīnagacītācik gītwām gīnātamak. That's what they did.

It was better, I think, that what they did before to make a living. They would rather fish and trap like before they went to war. This is what they were skilled at; they went back to it. That's what they did.

KC: Namwāc māga gīyociwētan ēwako pimācīsowin. Tāpiskōc anigi cīmāna kāgīyāpacītācik. Gīgasigana anigi otāwatāso cīmāna.

It was not easy that way of life. Just like those canoes they used. Those were heavy freighter canoes.

ES: Namwāc gīyociwētan.

It was not easy.

KC: Ēgwa mīna kāwotāpāstimēyan ocitaw pogo kamaskawācsiyan. Mōna na mosciwak kagīnēsōn.

When you drive dogs, you have to be strong. Not at all can you be weak.

ES: Ēh ēh, gīmaskawācsiyak anigi.

Yes, they were strong, them.

Māga ēgwa it took a lot out of them. Wīpac anigi gīpōnipimātisiwak. Awasimēwīs sixty years old ita kāgīnagataskēcik. Pēyagwan wīsta Jim.

But then it took a lot out of them. Soon they had died. Just over sixty years old when they left the Earth. It was the same for Jim.

We also spoke about my father.

KC: Ēgwāni ispīk kāgintē gowigawāyāk hospitalihk mitoni omisi ētastēnihk owīgwāgan ēgīpāgītinik otāpiskan. Ēgwa anōcīgē kāgīpamiyīt piponok anta Regina. Kītwām gīpēgīwēw ēgwa kātisīgwanik gīpītigēw hospital Nīpawawinihk. Āsay otēyāspinēt. Nigīgoyigawānān: nīna, nisīmis Clifford egwa Ordean Goulet. Ēgwāni iskowānīk kigawāpamak ēpimācsit. Ōma masinahigan kāmasināmān kanisitōtēn sēmāk ōma kāgītāt nigāwīpan, "Anawāc gīpamīcigātēnik otē mīna owīgwāgan."

It was when we visited him in the hospital; it was set way to the side, his face—his jaw had dropped. It was not long ago, the previous winter, they fixed his face in Regina. He came back home, and in the spring he went into the hospital in Nipawin. He already

*had heart problems. We visited him there: me, my
younger brother Clifford, and Ordean Goulet. That
was the last time I saw him alive. In this book I am
writing, you will understand right away what my
late mother said about him, "They should have fixed
his heart instead of his face."*

ES: Tāpwe anima gīpamīcigātēnik otē nōmagēs kiyāpic
kagīpimātsīta. Nīsta nigīyayān heart attack māga
gipamītāwak nite. Ēgota oci nigītiminowayān.

*That's true, if they had fixed his heart, he could have
lived a little longer. I, too, had a heart attack, but
they fixed my heart. From there, I got better health.*

KC: He could have lived a little longer.

ES: [Looking at his picture] Tāpwē naspitawēw Rogera.

Does he ever look like Roger [my dad's brother].

KC: Roger otānsa Beverly misāgamik ayāw pictures
her dad took and pictures they took of her dad,
Roger Carriere.

*Roger's daughter Beverly has many pictures
her dad took and pictures they took of her dad,
Roger Carriere.*

ES: Kistēs John māna mīcētwāw nigēcimik
French anima kayāsi nigamowin kāgīnagamot
kāgīyopāpāyān. Mistahi māna Roger gīpapāmi
cigāstēpicigēw.

*Your brother John, many times he asks me about
that old French song that was sung by my late*

*father. A whole lot as usual; Roger went around
taking pictures.*

*We were looking at a photograph of my uncle Roger wearing
a hooded and beaded moosehide jacket at the King Trapper
events in The Pas Trappers' Festival, circa 1960.*

KC: Anigi King Trapper events, Roger kāgīgiskāk
ēmīgistawigātēnik mosopāgwēgini miskotāgay.
Awina kāgīyosītamawāt?

*The King Trapper events, Roger is wearing a beaded
moosehide jacket. Who made it for him?*

ES: Marie Alma anima kāgīgasigwātāk asici
ēgīmīgistawāk.

*[It was] Marie Alma who stitched and beaded
it. [Marie Alma was Elise and my father's
sister, my aunt.]*

*We then looked at photographs of Charlie Budd, Medric
Poirier's barge service. Both men were from Sturgeon Landing
on Namew Lake (see the chapter "No Fear, Stay Calm").*

ES: Medric Poirier was handling freight from The Pas
to Sturgeon Landing. He also hauled fish to The Pas
from Namew Lake. Mistahi gīpimāgamigisiw. He
was always busy.

KC: Amisk Lake nimāmā otācimowin. Ēwago ana
Iskwēw, otāwiya kāgīmīnāt nimosom Dougal
McKenziewa, kawīgimānit. Ayāw oci, inigok
misāgamik awāsisa ēgīyāwāt ēgīwātisinit
Dougaliwa. Gītēpagēnimo kawīgimāt ēgwa
kigawīciyāt ēyopigināwasonit. Ēgwīni māga wīsta

gīnipawigo āgosiwin asici ocawāsimisa. They all had tuberculosis, commonly known as consumption. It had taken their lives.

At Beaver Lake, my mother's own story. This was of the woman whose father gave my grandfather Dougal McKenzie to marry. [My mother's story relates to her stepmother, Christiana Cursiteur.] The reason given is that there were so many orphaned children who came there to live with Dougal, she agreed to marry him and to help raise his children. However, she, too, died from the sickness along with her children. They all had tuberculosis, commonly known as consumption. It had taken their lives.

ES: Mīcēt gīnipahigok iskwēwak ēgwa awāsisak.

Many died from it, both women and children.

KC: Ōma otācimowin. This is my mother's story of Amisk Lake.

ES: You write it in Cree.

KC: Yes, with English translation.

ES: Nigīpōsin cimānis mēgwāc school holidays ēgospīk māna ēgīsicisawgawiyān Marie Alma kantēwīcāmagik.

I rode in a canoe during school holidays that time; usually, I was sent to Marie Alma to live with them.

KC: I told her Mom's story of John Budd. Mom found him to be quite funny.

John Budd, an elder and legendary figure in the Cumberland House region, circa 1950s. It seems likely that my uncle Roger Carriere and John Budd knew each other. John is wearing a railway engineer's hat in the photograph; Roger worked for CN Rail on the line from The Pas to Lynn Lake, Manitoba, for over thirty-five years.

Photo from Roger Carriere's collection, courtesy of Beverly Carriere, Cranberry Portage, Manitoba.

ES: I knew John Budd. Wīna ēgwa Albert Flett Rogera gīsinīgātēwak Apītawgosisān, halfbreed.

I knew John Budd. Him and Albert Flett called Roger a halfbreed.

KC: This picture of John Budd shows him wearing a railroad worker's hat.

ES: Āpō itigwē Roger ēgītōtamawāt.

It must have been Roger who brought it to him.

KC: Gīsāgiyēwīcēwēw anigi John Budda Roger?

Did Roger like the company of John Budd?

ES: Ēh ēh, ēgīsāgiyēwīcēwāt.

Yes, he enjoyed his company.

KC: This is a picture of Daniel Cook.

ES: Ninistawinēn ōma napagigamigos ōta cigāstēpiciganīk. Nigīpītigwān ōma wāskahiganis. Number Three Lake ōma kāgīyastēk.

I recognize that low-roofed cabin in this picture. I went in this cabin. Number Three Lake, that is where it stood.

KC: Wānaw na oci Egg Lake?

Was it far from Egg Lake?

ES: Wānawis.

Daniel Cook in front of his trapper's cabin, Napagamigos, skinning a muskrat caught during the spring trapping season in 1961. He was a trapper and fisherman who was nearly blind and who lived in Pemmican Portage with his family.

Photo from the Ron Mackay Collection, Northern Saskatchewan Archives, La Ronge, Saskatchewan.

A bit far.

KC: Manitoba border ētigwē? Ēgintē wacaskowanīgēyēk?

Maybe at the Manitoba border? You went there to trap muskrats?

ES: Māskōc gisiwak Shoal Lake anima kāgīcimatēk. Nīstanān ēgotē ēgīwanīgēyāk. Pagwānigamigohk niyanān ēgota gisiwak kāgīcimatāyāk anima pagwānigamik.

Maybe closer to Shoal Lake is where it stood. We, too, were there to trap. In a canvas tent, close to there is where we raised that canvas tent.

KC: Awina ēgota kāgīwīcāmat?

Who did you live there with?

ES: Simeon, āsay ēgīwīgītowak married already. Kayās
ōma oci waskahiganis.

*Simeon, we were married already. Long ago this
cabin was here.*

KC: Ayāw asici nigīyācimostāk nistēs Franklin. Ōma
otācimowin kīstawāw ēgīpiponi pagitawāyēk Sasagi
Sāgahiganihk. Anta māna pagitawāyin Fosterihk
isinīgātew.

*He also told me a story, my brother Franklin. In
this story, he told me you, too, winter fished at
Suggi Lake. It was there at the fishery, Foster's it
was called.*

ES: Āsay awāsisak nigīyāwānānak. We already
had children. Plenihk nigīpōsinān ēgotē
ēgītāstimigawiyāk. We rode in a plane; there is where
we were flown. Eddie ēgwa Mary nigīpēsiyāwak.

*My children, Eddie and Mary, I brought with me. Two
were left behind, Laurie and Caroline with "Big Man"
Edward Sayese, to keep them at home.*

KC: Fosterihk anima wīstawaw Marie Alma ēgwa John
Morin gīpagitawāyak. Piponi pagitawāyin ōma
kāmiskōtamāk.

*At Foster's there, them too, Marie Alma and
John Morin, had fished. It is winter fishing we are
talking about.*

ES: Tāpwē winter fishing ōma kāgītōtamāk.

True, winter fishing is what we did.

KC: Nipāpā wīstawāw ēgwa Franklin ēgota gīpagitawāyak.

My dad, them too, and Franklin, there they fished.

ES: Ayāwa gīwīcēwēw Franklina asici Johnny Poirierwa [Johnny Dorion].

He went with Franklin and Johnny "Poirier" Dorion.

KC: Franklin otācimowin: "Itayitē namwāc mistahi kagācitināgok kinosēwak sēmāk nigīyācipagitawānān. Ēgwa mīna inigok kāgācitināgok kinosēwak nigītāskītwātonān kāyisimāmawiyāk."

Franklin's story: "Where we didn't catch many fish right away, we moved our nets. Then, too, all of the fish we caught, we would split them among everyone."

ES: Ēgosi kāgītōtāgik. That's what they did. They split everything they caught. Even when groceries came in, they split everything too.

KC: Tāpwē isa kāgītagāgīcik.

That for sure was a good move.

ES: Mitoni māga. Without a doubt. They split everything evenly.

KC: [Some of the] pictures in this memoir book are now kept in a library at Air Ronge, Saskatchewan. Other

Photo of Aunt Elise Sayese at her home in The Pas, with her orphaned grand-daughter, Lilleniy "Lily" Hunter, who lives with her.

Photo by Ken Carriere, March 16, 2020.

pictures I will put in this book are from Roger's photo collection.

I then showed my aunt the photograph of my grandfather Dougal's father, "Old" Bill McKenzie, who had come to this country from Scotland (see the chapter "Where Prayers Are Called Upon" and "Margaret Schweitzer Interview").

ES: Nigīwāpamaw ēwago ("Old" Bill McKenzie) ana gīwīcāmēw kimāmāwa. Gītagopiciw ēgotē.

I saw him, that "Old" Bill McKenzie. He lived with your mom. He came to live with her there.

KC: Tānspīk ōma?

When was this?

ES: In the 1940s.

KC: From Margaret Schweitzer's story: Cumberland ana micētwaw gitohtēwo.

From Margaret Schweitzer's story: Cumberland was where he went to many times.

ES: Kimāmā ana māna kāgīpamiyāt ēgotē Cumberland.

It was your mom who always took care of him in Cumberland House.

Appendix:

A GUIDE TO SWAMPY CREE PRONUNCIATION

———◇———

Standard Roman Orthography (SRO) written symbols for Swampy Cree are as follows.

CONSONANTS

c	the ch sound in *chum, mooch*
g	*get, igloo*
h	*happy, ah*
k	*karate, okay*
m	*me, him*
n	*net, an*
p	*poem, up*
s	*sill, must*
t	*to, it*
w	*watt, slow*

VOWELS AND SEMI-VOWELS

a, A	sounds like the u in *mud* or *bud*
wa	wa in *walk*
ya	ya in *Maya, yard*
aw	aw in *awake, awash*
ay	ay in *Ayatollah*

ā, Ā sounds like the a in *sad, Sam, jam*
  wā wa in *water, wag, wad*
  yā ya in *yahoo, yard, yam*
  āw aw in *awkward, awning, awl*
  āy ay in *aye, Ayurveda*

ē, Ē sounds like the e in *red, led, fed*
  wē we in *wet, web, wed*
  yē ye in *yell, yet, yen*
  ēw makes a sound similar to the English combination ay-oo
  ēy ay in *pray, may, day*

i, I sounds like the i in *mitt, sit, bit*
  wi wi in *wing, wit, wink*
  yi yi in *yippee, yield*
  iw makes a sound similar to the English combination ee-oo
  iy an abrupt īy and sounds like i in *tick*, used for noun endings

ī, Ī sounds like the e in *me, be*
  wī wee in *weed*, wea in *weave, wean*
  yī yea in *year, yeast*
  īw ew in *ewe, sewer*
  īy ee in *meet*, ea in *teach*

o, O sounds like the oo in *good, stood, wood*
  wo wo in *wolf*, woo in *wool* and *woof*
  yo yo in *yolk*
  ow ow in *know, snow, grow*
  oy oy in *buoy* and in *boy* approximate to the ōy sound

ō, Ō	sounds like the oo in *boot, root, loot*
wō	oo in *woo*, o in *woke*
yō	you in *you*, yo in *yoga*, yoo in *yoo-hoo*
ōw	ow in *own, owe*
ōy	oy in *oyster*

Sources for phonetic sounds of Swampy and Plains Cree approximate to English wording:

Fergusson, Rosalind. *Penguin Pocket Rhyming Dictionary*. Aylesbury, UK: Market House Books, 2006.

Wolfart, H. Christoph, and Janet F. Caroll. *Meet Cree*. Edmonton: University of Alberta Press, 1981.

Wolvengrey, Arok. *nēhiyawēwin: itwēwina/Cree: Words*. Vol. 1. Regina: Canadian Plains Research Center, 2001.

SUGGESTED READING

———————◇———————

Acco, Anne. *Ekosi: A Métisse Retrospective of Poetry and Prose.* Saskatoon: Gabriel Dumont Institute, 2009.

Bird, Louis. *The Spirit Lives in the Mind: Omushkego Stories, Lives, and Dreams.* Compiled and edited by Susan Elaine Gray. Montreal and Kingston: McGill-Queen's University Press, 2007.

Black Hawk. *Life of Black Hawk, or Ma-ka-tai-me-she-kia-kiak, Dictated by Himself.* Edited with an introduction and notes by J. Gerald Kennedy, assisted by Anthony Hoefer. New York: Penguin Books, 2008.

Columbo, John Robert, ed. *Windigo: An Anthology of Fact and Fantastic Fiction.* Saskatoon: Western Producer Prairie Books, 1982.

Dickason, Olive P. *The Myth of the Savage and the Beginnings of French Colonialism in the Americas.* Edmonton: University of Alberta Press, 1997.

Dobbin, Murray. *The One-and-a-Half Men: The Story of Jim Brady and Malcolm Norris, Métis Patriots of the 20th Century.* Vancouver: New Star Books, 1981.

Garvin, Terry. *Bush Land People.* Calgary: Arctic Institute of North America, University of Calgary, 1992.

Suggested Reading

Hearne, Samuel. *Journals of Samuel Hearne and Philip Turnor*. Edited with an introduction and notes by J.B. Tyrrell. Toronto: Champlain Society, 1934.

Henry, Alexander. *Travels and Adventures in Canada and the Indian Territories between the Years 1760 and 1776*. Boston: Little, Brown, 1901.

Keighley, Sydney Augustus, in collaboration with Renée Fossett Jones and David Kirkby Riddle. *Trader, Tripper, Trapper: The Life of a Bay Man*. Winnipeg: Rupert's Land Research Centre in cooperation with Watson and Dwyer, 1989.

Littlejohn, Cathy. *Métis Soldiers of Saskatchewan: 1914–1953*. Saskatoon: Gabriel Dumont Institute, 2012.

Lytwyn, Victor P. *Muskekowuck Athinuwick: Original People of the Great Swampy Land*. Winnipeg: University of Manitoba Press, 2002.

Malcolm, Andrew H. "Through Canada's North by Dogsled." *New York Times*, September 13, 1981. https://www.nytimes.com/1981/09/13/travel/through-canada-s-north-by-dogsled.html.

Preston, Richard J. *Cree Narrative: Expressing the Personal Meanings of Events*. 2nd ed. Montreal and Kingston: McGill-Queen's University Press, 2002.

Thompson, David. *David Thompson's Narrative of His Explorations in Western America, 1784–1812*. Edited by J.B. Tyrrell. Toronto: Champlain Society, 1916.

Thoreau, Henry David. *Walden and Other Writings of Henry David Thoreau*. Edited with an introduction by Joseph Wood Krutch. New York: Bantam Books, 1989.

Watkins, E.A., J.A. Mackay, and R. Faries. *A Dictionary of the Cree Language: As Spoken by the Indians in the Provinces of Quebec, Ontario, Manitoba, Saskatchewan and Alberta*. Toronto: General Synod of the Church of England in Canada, 1938.

Wolvengrey, Arok. *nēhiyawēwin: itwēwina/Cree: Words*. Vols. 1 and 2. Regina: Canadian Plains Research Center, 2011.

PHOTO: Courtesy of Ken Carriere.

A retired educator, geologist, trapper, commercial fisher, and tourist guide, KEN CARRIERE is a fluent speaker of the Swampy Cree dialect and a member of the Peter Ballantyne Cree Nation in northeastern Saskatchewan. He currently resides in the northern Saskatchewan village of Air Ronge.